Healing From Infidelity

A Practical Guide to Healing from Infidelity and How to Help Your Partner to Heal from Your Affair

By: Jackson A. Thomas - Debbie Lancer

Table of Contents

Introduction 1
Chapter 1: Defining Infidelity 2
Chapter 2: Even Happy People Cheat 12
Chapter 3: Monogamy and Its Discontents 16
Chapter 4: Why Being Betrayed Hurts so Much 21
Chapter 5: Jealousy 23
Chapter 6: The Two Sides of the Affair – the Betrayed and the Cheater 28
Chapter 7: Tell or Not to Tell? 33
Chapter 8: Vengeance 40
Chapter 9: Is Sex Just Sex? 47
Chapter 10: After the Affair 51
Chapter 11: Become Sexual Again 60
Chapter 12: The Man and Woman Difference 69
Chapter 13: Rebuilding Trust 74
Chapter 14: Dealing with Your Partner Obsession 77
Chapter 15: How to Change from Destroyer to Healer .. 79
Chapter 16: Healing from an Affair/Infidelity, Together or Apart 81
Conclusion 91

Introduction

Congratulations and thank you for downloading *Healing from Infidelity: A Practical Guide to Healing from Infidelity and How to Help Your Partner to Heal from Your Affair*. In today's world, infidelity is one of the main tragedies that can befall a relationship. Majority of the people who find themselves in this situation do not know how to move past the betrayal and pain. Healing can be a hard and complicated process after a person is betrayed by a loved one.

Downloading this book is the first step you can take towards healing and becoming better in your relationship. If you have decided to forego the relationship, you still need healing, and this book will also help you. The first step is always the easiest; however, which is why the information you find in the following chapters is very important to take to heart. The concepts you find herein can be put to action immediately or at a later date depending on your situation.

There are plenty of books on this subject on the market, thanks again for choosing this one! Every effort was made to ensure it is full of as much useful information as possible. The language used herein is simple so that everyone can get the help he/she needs, please enjoy!

Chapter 1: Defining Infidelity

Infidelity is one of the greatest tragedies that befall relationships. When we are young, relationships are easy, and love is simple. Love at a young age consists of loving parents, best friends, and peers. There are hardly any complications and serious obligations arising with the word love when one is young. However, as we get older and settle in serious relationships consisting of spouses and long-term commitment, the words love and intimacy get more complicated; they come with expectations and commitments. We are expected to meet the needs of our partners as they ensure that our needs are also met.

The biggest challenge with infidelity is that most couples do not discuss the issue in details. As such, it becomes hard to define it because everyone has different expectations. Normally, infidelity and cheating are words used to mean the same thing. Some couples will consider flirting with other people as cheating while others may not. Cheating can also be considered as follows:

- Discussing sexual things with other people apart from their partners
- Chatting online with other people
- Sharing emotional and personal emotions with other people
- Having sexual contact with other people

Some couples have no problem with the acts mentioned above, and in fact, some find it okay to have sexual relations with others while in a relationship with their spouses. Other couples will find every one of the above acts as offensive as they can get. Whether it is emotional, physical, or cyber-based cheating, only an individual in the relationship can define for themselves the unacceptable behavior. The only real way of defining infidelity and cheating is if a spouse feels his/her expectations were not met by the partner (related to sexual and emotion-related contact with other people). When the expectations of the individual have been violated, then the emotional outcome is betrayal. If a spouse has feelings of betrayal, then yes, the partner might be cheating.

Defining Infidelity in a Relationship

How can one define infidelity in a relationship? Here, the spouses might have a challenge. Typically, when we talk about infidelity, we refer to sexual affairs. It is true to say that sexual affairs are the most destructive form of cheating and infidelity, but there are other ways people become unfaithful in relationships and marriages. Emotional cheating involves getting too close to someone other than your spouse to the extent that you lose interest in the primary relationship. Emotional infidelity can be online or face-to-face but without sexual contact.

Some acts that we consider small might lead to huge infidelity actions. It is therefore important that we safeguard our relationships. Most couples will avoid discussing infidelity in details for various reasons. First, in the initial stages of a relationship, the partners might feel too in love hence overlook the impact of cheating and infidelity in their commitment. Again, a couple might avoid bringing the topic up in fear that one person will misinterpret the other as untrusting.

A couple might express to each other that cheating is unacceptable but then fail to describe what cheating is in their terms. Consequently, one person might consider chatting with strangers as a good thing while the other finds it offensive, and since there is no absolute definition, the couples will disagree.

It is important for couples to sit and agree on what is inappropriate and appropriate behavior. Such a discussion cannot be easy, but at least you will have a common ground to work from together. Be ready to have different views on the topic, but the best thing is to come to a common ground. There are things one partner may mention, and the other feels like they are overreactions, but the two people need to understand the needs of each other. Everyone needs to realize that no matter what their feelings towards a particular topic, the other person may not see the weight, therefore, can dismiss the suggestion and even fail to change accordingly. In such a case, you will be required to decide whether you can live with the person or not.

Typically, infidelity is defined as the violation of a sexual agreement between two people in a relationship. Under the Romanticism philosophy, sex is not just a physical act; instead, it includes the central symbol and summation of love. Since the mid-eighteenth century, the romanticism philosophy has been the human understanding of love. Before this philosophy came to life, people fell in love and had sex, but they did not see these two acts as having a shared link. People could have sex and not love while others could love and not get intimate. The philosophy of romanticism puts sex as the crowning moment of love whereby one expresses his/her devotion for the other through physical, sexual encounters.

The romanticism philosophy turned infidelity into a catastrophic event because we can no longer separate sex with love. In other words, sex was as a result of intense and profound desire to commit to a person. It is hard to assume that sex meant nothing between two people. Thus, when we discover that our partner cheated, we link emotions, feelings, desires, and the need to commit. Consequently, we feel that the person is no longer in love with us but is seeking for ways to spend their life with the other. We feel like the affection of our partner towards us has dropped. This assumption is not necessarily true.

There are, of course, several cases whereby infidelity means that a person has contempt for his/her relationship and is looking for someone else; however, that is not always the truth. In some events, infidelity means something else. For instance, it could be a passing emotion, a short-term desire for erotic excitement, or a feeling that co-exists with the sincere commitment to a life partner.

Our culture and general upbringing have made it almost impossible for us to separate love and things we term as infidelity; thus, it is hard to get over an act of cheating. Although several people have gotten past the romanticism philosophy and can easily separate love and cheating, the majority of us still hold onto the idea that the two are intertwined. It has become a challenge of great proportions and even brute impossibility to separate the unfaithful act from the person. However much a spouse spends time explaining to a partner that the act of infidelity meant nothing, it seems impossible. How can sex, private chatting, or any act of cheating mean anything less than everything?

Summarily, we can say that there might be a simple way of getting out of the impasse. Maybe, if we could conduct a frank examination of the lines of one's mind, and maybe an honest remembrance of certain moments of personal experiences, we might find it easier to separate love and infidelity, therefore, healing easily. A brave investigation of the mind might reveal that every person is capable in a rather strange and surprising way to care deeply for someone and at the same time entertain or mastermind a sexual scenario with someone else. However, the thought seems impossible when it comes from the mouth of a cheating partner–loving one person and engaging another sexually.

Considering the philosophy of romanticism, we can argue that it would be easier for us to recover from the wounds of infidelity if we ignore romanticism. If we let go of the thought that infidelity has to mean something more than just physical interest, we might have an easier time healing from these cases. What if we let go of the mentality we currently have and consult other sources of information such as our own experiences? We should look at our mental formations when we last thought of infidelity. The pain of being cheated on will most definitely be there, but then it will be easier to forgive and even understand the actions of our partners. Putting yourself in the shoes of a spouse may help you understand or even accept the apology of our partner. If we base our thoughts of infidelity on subjective experiences, we may be able to redemptively soften, forgive, and even forget what happens when we become victims.

The questions arise: what causes infidelity and why do we feel so hurt when betrayed?

Causes of Infidelity

Certain things lead to infidelity. They can be classified into but not limited to physical, emotional, and practical causes.

Physical Causes

Some of the partners engaging in acts of infidelity cite sexual dissatisfaction with their partners. They state that their reason for straying is that sex is not as they would expect so they tend to feel unfulfilled. The straying partners may state that they do not receive enough pleasure or even reach the climax as they would like. In other cases, they might state a lack of passion and chemistry as their reason for infidelity. In the latter case, the straying spouse might be comparing their current sex to what they had when the relationship was starting. Normally, sex in the initial stages of a relationship is wild, exciting, and liberated; therefore, couples can misconstrue the honeymoon phase sex as passion and chemistry.

Consequently, a person may be tempted to look for that passion and fire in a new partner instead of identifying ways to relight the chemistry in his/her relationship. Seeking sexual satisfaction outside a relationship just because it is boring or different from the expectation is like engaging in drugs, gambling, shopping, and other quick fix options to escape reality. You will still have to look at real life, the causes, and the consequences. The belief that having sex with someone who does not know you allow a certain level of freedom which lacks in a formal relationship also fuels infidelity. The need for hot and free sex with an anonymous person is also another reason that people give when they are engaging in infidelity.

Emotional Causes

One of the most mentioned and blamed causes of infidelity are an emotional disconnection from a spouse. A person engaging in infidelity will sight having felt unappreciated and sad in the relationship, therefore, was looking for consolation outside. Emotional disconnection can lead to secondary feelings such as resentment and anger, hence leading to both emotional and physical affairs. An emotional affair may appear like a friendship at first but gradually develops into serious levels of intimacy where more personal information gets shared. Information about unhappiness and dissatisfaction in the primary relationship might become an integral part of such a friendship. The 'friend' takes on a serious role in the plans of the partner and mostly becomes a substitute in the plans, thoughts, and fantasies of the other.

Practical Causes

Over the years, most people have started questioning the practicality of the philosophy of romanticism. A good number of people from the younger generation have questioned the practicality of monogamy and its benefits. Consequently, they are choosing relationships and lifestyles that are less monogamous. However, such choices have brought on challenges as there lacks a clear roadmap on having open relationships. People in open relationships have their own set of rules, and if one person deviates from them, it brings on feelings of betrayal and hurt. The unfortunate part for couples believing in polygamy is that they make a lot of mistakes when applying their rules.

Does infidelity mean the end of a relationship or love?

Infidelity will give different results for different people. Some relationships will come to an end, while others will thrive. Other couples will tolerate the hurt but might never thrive. The results depend on the individuals and the cause. For some relationships, the spouses will find a reason to turn everything around and start a fresh commitment, while others will find this as a cause for separation. Either way, most of the relationships ending because of infidelity have other underlying factors that are unresolvable. Ending the relationship will cause a lot of heartaches, but if it is the best option for the two people, then they have to accept it. However, choosing to heal the relationship and move on will take time, brutal honesty, reflection, and mighty dedication from both people.

Is infidelity the only hurtful thing in a relationship?
No, infidelity is not the only thing that breaks relationships. Typically, affairs will cause devastating emotions and results in relationships, but they are not the main way of destroying what you have. When one assesses the causes of infidelity, he/she will realize that an affair is just a symptom of breakage as well as a cause. There are thousands of other ways through which people break their relationships for instance through withholding affection, love, failing to approve one another, being judgmental in a negative way, or criticizing each other every time. Almost everyone in a relationship, regardless of how committed and loving they are, will do one of these relationship breaking things. We should pay attention to our spouses so that we can notice when their needs and patterns change.

How does infidelity happen?

First, infidelity/cheating is a devastating act of betrayal. However, it can also be a sign of loss, loneliness, and the need for autonomy, novelty, intimacy, power, affection, or the need to be loved, desired, and wanted. All these needs are valid and important. They do not represent a lack of self-reliance or neediness in any way. They are the reason we come together, fall in love, and choose to stay with our partners, but also the main reasons we fall out of love.

The best part of a human being is visible when we are connected with other people, especially the ones we love, adore, and feel connected to wholesomely. The human need for connection, love, intimacy, and validation are very primal. They are hard-wired into us and cannot be ignored, denied, or pushed down. They can never disappear. Consequently, if these needs are left unmet for too long, the relationship will experience a tear wide enough for someone else to walk in and claim the chance to meet those needs. If a stranger starts meeting any of these important needs, an intimacy, alchemy, desire, and attraction will grow—for the intruder.

When a person has an important need that is unmet for too long, there are only two options—and I mean only two. The person either lets go of the need completely or changes the environment to meet it, which applies to every human being. If the need is subtle, then we can ignore it; if it is basic, then we have to meet it, one way or another. This will create a rift in the relationship. Hence the real temptation to change the conditions, as in find another person to meet the needs we would like our partners to settle.

Affairs are not usually about wanting the intruder, rather, the way they meet the needs. If the person having an affair had a choice, it would be to have his/her partner meet the need, instead of the intruder. The cheater does not want to hurt the spouse—that is why they do it in secret. However, life is complicated, and things do not always work out the way we want. Needs get demanding, and the desire to cheat gets heightened. When an affair happens, chances are one of the following three things have happened:

- Something is missing in the relationship, but the partners are not aware of what it is.
- Something is missing, and a person knows exactly what it is; for instance, a need has been hungry for too long, but the two people lack openness and honesty in the relationship.
- There are repeated attempts to state the unmet needs, but they are all unsuccessful; thus, the spouse has to look for comfort from outside.

Sometimes, the needs are not as a result of weaknesses in the relationship, rather, dissatisfaction within the self. Some people cheat even when they are in a happy relationship.

Chapter 2: Even Happy People Cheat

The general thought is that infidelity affects only broken relationships and dysfunctional homes. However, this is not always the case. A good number of people in relationships we would term as "perfect" also find themselves cheating.

Mitchell, a work colleague asked me if I knew a good therapist or marriage counselor. I told her I knew a few and would recommend one depending on the issue. It had not occurred to me that she was looking for help for herself because her life looked quite perfect. She confided in me that although she has a happy home, good kids, lovely family, financial stability, an amazing husband, and everything one could wish for in a relationship, she was cheating. To make matters worse, she was cheating with a guy who had no job, not as handsome as the husband, and so many other lacking things. It came as a surprise to me, and I recommended a therapist. However, I was left wondering, what makes one cheat on a committed partner and put a happy home at risk?

The general thought for such cheating is that the cheater or the relationship has some hidden problems. Some therapists explain that such cheaters might have some unresolved trauma from childhood or previous relationships, or there is some form of attachment dysfunction. People also define such acts as emotional immaturity pushing a person to certain acts. Other times, we assume that there are some significant but hidden flaws in the primary relationship, and the affected person do not know how to address it. However, we look at it, infidelity is viewed as a symptom of underlying and unsolved problems. Cheating is, in most cases, a result of troubled relationships, may it be open or hidden.

Interestingly, such assumptions have proved to be true for a large number of people seeking help for infidelity. Some people cheat because of attachment disorders, while others are using illicit sexual and emotional affairs to deal with traumas from their childhood. Some people will use infidelity to distract themselves from reality as is the case with people using drugs and other distractors. Sometimes, a relationship can be working well, but one partner feels unsatisfied therefore looks for a reason to break up. In other cases, the relationship might be doing very well, but one partner feels a void and looks for sexual satisfaction outside (such as one-night stand) to feel alive.

However, the reasons mentioned above do not explain the cause and effect for everyone who is in a happy relationship and still cheating. There are some people who explain that they are happy in their relationship, their sex life is great, there are no financial challenges or other home challenges that might lead to cheating, but they cheat anyway. Some do not want to stop and others just can't because it gives them some sense of power.

So, the cheating partner is there, happy in the primary relationship but also looking for pleasure outside through infidelity. Interestingly, the cheating spouse will look for a reason to justify his/her actions even when there is none. You will find such a person saying "Surely, there is something wrong with my relationship, otherwise, I would not be cheating." And typically, when they engage a therapist, he/she will start searching for underlying problems.

In my study of sex and intimacy issues in relationships, I have learned that infidelity might be a symptom of challenges in the relationship, but it is not always so. Some people cheat because they can and do not want to stop. Others are reasonably healthy but still choose to stray from the primary relationship. This applies to both men and women.

There are several reasons why a person in a good relationship might still choose to cheat even if they are in a healthy and happy relationship.

Firstly, a person can engage in cheating for self-exploration purposes. While some people might have explored a lot and are not interested in anymore exploiting, some are still searching for a new sense of life in themselves. In all reasons for cheating while in a happy home, affairs as a form of 'discovery' has kept turning up. People may use infidelity 'to falsely discover' their identity. For the people engaging in infidelity for the self-discovery reason, there is rarely a problem in the reason, and they do not see the need to quit the cheating habit. They see cheating as an expansive experience involving exploration, growth, and transformation.

Cheaters will also describe their practices as a way of discovering repressed parts of self. It is fuel to moving from the current self to a new and better person. Surprisingly, when looked at closely, these people do not want to change from who they are to someone else. All they seek is an escape from their ordinary self for a short while. Some seek to feel young again; others seek unburdened sex, while others want fun. Researches show that these people are not looking for a new person when they cheat, rather, they are looking for themselves.

Secondly, a person may cheat to fulfill the allure of a life not lived. A spouse may be drawn into cheating by a life not lived. Missed opportunity may make a person want to try out what they never had. For instance, a person may meet the one that got away years after he/she is married and chooses to engage in the act of infidelity. Again, a person might have gotten into the current primary relationship half willingly; for instance, maybe the woman got pregnant without the right preparations. This relationship may make the person feel as if he/she is closed in and limited to certain things. To feel free, these spouses may opt to indulge their curiosity and see who they would have been if they had not settled for the current partner. Such infidelity introduces the individual to the stranger within.

Thirdly, a person may choose to cheat because of the attractive nature of the transgression. Some happy people who cheat explain that they feel like teenagers when sneaking around and cheating, therefore, will do it for the thrill. The fact that cheating is forbidden makes it exciting, and some people get the kick out of defying the rules. More like a child sneaking a cookie which the parent said he/she could not have, the cheating spouses feel that the stolen fruit is sweeter. The seductive nature of transgression can be defined as the excitement coming from attraction overcoming obstacles. Just as the children and teens push limits to discover their ability, self, and the world, the adults engaging in infidelity may find the forbidden more thrilling.

Fourthly, a happy person may cheat to revive some exiled emotions or find new ones. This desire falls under the need to discover. It is a form of self-discovery, and men are more susceptible to this need. As the men grow up, they are taught to suppress their emotions and avoid expressing them. Consequently, they learn to stifle pain, as well as joy, the good and the bad. Regardless of gender, any person can use infidelity as an emotional release platform rather than sexual.

Cheating hurts no matter the reason. A person who is cheated on will feel betrayed regardless of the reason the other spouse gives. There is no good reason to cheat mainly if one chose the partner and made promises to stay with him/her only. However, reasons for cheating matter when a person goes for therapy because they help to understand the best approach to healing.

Chapter 3: Monogamy and Its Discontents

Many cultures have sanctioned monogamy and upheld it as the center of civilization. However, there are some aspects of civilization that have not been understood completely. Everyone is aware, either completely or vaguely, that monogamy produces a social contract that is peaceful to a large extent supporting a framework for economic advancement and cultural harmony. Still, this realization has not been studied extensively. There lacks a comprehensive report on why we settle for monogamy while there are other options.

And like every other hard-won battle, monogamy is not a perfect choice for everyone. Whence examined closely, we can realize there are a good number of private dissatisfactions in monogamy. These imperfections form a nagging undercurrent of discomfort in any culture. Under ordinary circumstances, these dissatisfactions are seen as a form of deviance and are generally disapproved and suppressed by the vast majority. However, they are impossible to eradicate from society. The only time that culture may experience some relief is if people begin to appreciate the weaknesses of monogamy and look at other possibilities.

The silent question in our society today is how much of anti-monogamy practices can we accommodate in the community before we lose our culture. A good number of people already appreciate the idea of open relationship; others are choosing to bear children out of wedlock, while others are taking divorce as a norm. There are some practices in the society that hold the ideology of monogamy since ancient time but have examined them as times are changing.

Polygamy persisted since time immemorial for both human beings and animals. However, as human beings became civilized, they reinvented monogamy. This reinvention did not do away with polygamy entirely because of the basic nature of mammals except a few animals such as orangutans, gibbons, and beavers. Over the centuries, the debate of monogamy versus polygamy has brought different results and opinions in people. However, monogamy has held the forefront.

What makes monogamy so successful and appreciated across cultures?

Firstly, it reduces sexual competition among the male species and creates a social contract. Looking at the animals, males do not have a fair chance to mate, rather, it is about strength and getting as many females as possible. With monogamy, however, there is the rationale that every male will get a chance to mate. Consequently, the do or die mating competition among men reduces. If one male can collect many females, then the competition becomes deadly intense. However, monogamy promises a democratic outcome, and the bachelor herd disappears.

Secondly, monogamy reassures everyone in the society that they have a chance to reproduce; therefore, another social contract develops. There is no risk of a certain group outcasting or pulling in people from other groups through reproduction. The society can function as a whole. Monogamy ensures that people can pair off for reproduction purposes, but they have to keep other social and familial relationships. Consequently, the community can cooperate. Monogamy also ensures that men and women can easily work together in non-sexual settings even though there is role tension as the world gets more complex.

Monogamy also ensures that we develop a complex personality allowing us to maintain sexual relationship privacy and at the same time maintain a multilayered network of friends, relatives, associates, acquaintances, strangers, and even coworkers who we interact with without sexual intentions unlike other mammals living in collective doubt.

We can, therefore, say that although monogamy has its discontents, distinct advantages are making it most viable for human beings. These advantages have a price.

In a monogamous setting, everyone has the chance to get a partner regardless of their status. A high-status woman does not have to worry about sharing her mate with a low-status woman, and a low-status man has a chance of getting a mate. In this case, status is defined as the quality of beauty, characteristic, strength, brightness, speed intelligence, and any other admirable character. With human males, there is a crucial character that women look for: the willingness to provide for the offspring.

Keeping all these factors in mind, let us account for the major areas of dissatisfaction with monogamy. First, the one-mate-per-person idea limits the mating urges of males. Naturally, male species have the underlying desire to mate with as many females as possible. The Coolidge effect explains that a barnyard male animal will get a resurge of sexual desire as soon as a new female is introduced into the barn even if it had just exhausted its energies.

Monogamy has resulted in serial monogamy, whereby a male or female changes partner as he/she moves up the ladder. Because a low-status person would probably be forced to mate with a person of the same level even if he/she is unsatisfied, one of the results is divorce, and marrying someone better as the standards rise. This effect is more visible in men who marry women who are way younger than them after leaving their wives and children. On the side of the woman agreeing to marry an older man, it is a case of choosing a man who can provide rather than a man who looks good yet cannot offer support for the offspring.

People who are unsatisfied with monogamy settle for other options such as single motherhood, divorces and remarrying, not marrying but having several partners in different locations, open relationships, et cetera. Male dissatisfaction with monogamy is normally very open, unlike female dissatisfaction.

Should we then accept a more practical alternative such as polygamy? That is, should we allow people to openly choose the side they want to settle in? This kind of freedom might open the world to acceptance, but it might also bring confusion. People will no longer be sure of whether their spouses will be monogamous for life or they will get to a point where they change their agenda.
To sum up, the above analysis shows clearly why monogamy is best suited for our society. Polygamy might bring in confusion and aggression as every mate tries to identify the best option. Monogamy is essential for humankind to keep the current family values. Most of the family values followed today is based on a husband, wife, and children setup which makes the human society progressive and peaceful. Practices challenging the monogamy contract such as divorce, legalized prostitution, pornography, single parenthood by choice, and homosexuality should be addressed because they pose a threat to the norm. If we accept anti-monogamy practices without real analysis and understanding, we might end up confused and non-progressive.

Polygamy might seem appealing for people unsatisfied by monogamy and may choose to support their cause, but they should take note: looking beyond the personal dissatisfaction, which we all might feel at one point or the other, we all have a responsibility of retaining a permanent stake at ensuring that the society remains peaceful and orderly. We should ensure that in the world, everybody has a reasonable and fair chance of achieving happiness. And although monogamy makes tough demands on us, it also offers complex and unique rewards to society.

Chapter 4: Why Being Betrayed Hurts so Much

According to studies, researches, and even personal experiences, infidelity can be defined simply as broken royalty or trust. As mentioned in the previous topic, there are things in a relationship that spouses consider sacred and a sign of royalty and trust. Acts such as sex are held high in a marriage and should only be done by the two people in love. If one person breaks such exclusive acts, the other spouse feels betrayed. Infidelity involves the violation of a stated or an assumed contract regarding sexual and emotional exclusivity. Some scholars define it as a violation by subjective feelings, whereby one feels that the partner has violated certain norms and consequently lead to feelings of jealousy and rivalry in the relationship.

In marriages and marital relationships, the expectations of exclusivity are assumed to be sexual and entire emotional feelings, although they are not always met. Researches have revealed that when these exclusive expectations are not met, the psychological damage can easily occur, including feelings of betrayal and rage, lowered feelings of sexual, battered personal confidence, lowered self-esteem, and even damage to self-image. The consequence violation of exclusivity acts is normally determined by the context. If the acts become public, the involved people might face social consequences. The extent and form of infidelity consequences are, in most cases, dependent on the gender of the accused person.

When considering reasons why infidelity hurts so much, we need to understand the nature of infidelity. An action that violates an explicit or implicit agreement between two people in a relationship therefore undermining the exclusivity of the commitment is infidelity. From the above definitions, acts of infidelity can be either physical or emotional. In most cases, dishonesty is part of infidelity, but that is not always the case. From my studies and experiences, infidelity is not a new thing. It is one of the main causes of couples seeking counsel and even separation. Infidelity, whether presumed, considered, or committed, signifies a crisis to most couples. The offender and the offended both get flooded with emotions and become fairly deregulated. The hurt is intense because the two spouses had high expectations for each other. Maybe one did not mean what he/she said when committing, but the other might have put all his/her commitment in the relationship.

Because of the intensity and weight attached to violation acts, infidelity takes a sit in the room like a third person, feeding on the strength of the relationship. The feelings of rage and anger grow, bringing in more confusion and fear, confidence and trust become shattered, and the openness between the two people varnishes. Infidelity feels like an object propelled in an otherwise well-flowing scene in a movie–like a grenade or a bomb. There is also a continuous feeling of loss. The lifespan of the relationship becomes divided into before and after–that is, before the infidelity and after the infidelity. The behavior of the spouses will be affected by cheating acts, and they may change noticeably and permanently. A lot of things in the relationship tend to change, both noticeably and invisibly. Some couples can repair their relationship and even take the brokenness as an opportunity to change, grow and reconnect while others cannot replace the broken trust, thus choose to leave the commitment.

Chapter 5: Jealousy

Jealousy is normally defined as the unpleasant emotion arising when an intruder encroaches on something that one feels is his/her own. Jealousy can be difficult and particularly frustrating to talk about with a spouse or anyone. Generally, jealousy in relationships is associated with romantically involved couples, but it can develop in any relationship and cause emotional distress and conflict. Majority of cultures encourage monogamous relationships, and jealousy will generally set in from suspicions or concerns that one partner is not faithful anymore. Jealousy can hinder the ability of a person to communicate if not addressed appropriately. Without effective and open communication, couples might even misinterpret the intentions and expectations of each other about the relationship. What is harmless to one person might be a threat to the relationship for another and without clear communications; no one will know the boundaries. Cultural perception of infidelity also affects the way jealousy is expressed. In most cases, women are expected to tolerate their men when they cheat. On the other hand, women are bashed, shamed, and judged harshly.

According to some researches, jealousy is difficult to define on its own, but it comprises of uncomfortable feelings such as betrayal, loss, abandonment, anger, and embarrassment. Further modern research has identified a connection between the attachment system of the brain and the primal nature of jealousy. The attachment system is very crucial in the process of social bonding and will act on external threats. Taking this into consideration, we can say that jealousy is a necessary evil that encourages the life of a relationship and also deters infidelity.

However, not all forms of jealousy are healthy. Certain studies revealed that excessive jealousy is positively correlated with instability. People with too much jealousy are less agreeable and emotionally unstable. This means that excessively jealous people will try to control the lives of their spouses, wanting to monitor who they spend time with, what they wear, and also look for ways to undermine their self-esteem.

It can be very hard to deal with a jealous partner especially if there is no real cause for the feelings. Normally, unnecessary jealousy stems from the feeling of inadequacy. Recent psychological researches have revealed that most people try to transfer their discomfort to others through anger; thus, the desperation to control the relationship as much as possible. Unfortunately, one partner will feel choked and look for ways to escape the pressure of the relationship. Excessive jealousy will do more harm than good.

Jealousy and Gender

According to a study conducted at Chapman University about infidelity, men and women differ when it comes to jealousy. The study was conducted on nearly 64,000 Americans examining how different genders react to infidelity (sexual vs. emotional infidelity). It was found that heterosexual men were more upset about sexual infidelity than heterosexual women. However, men are less likely to be upset about emotional infidelity compared to women.

Both sexual and emotional infidelity can result in harm for both men and women, including abrupt end of relationships, heartaches leading to violence, loss of resources, and broken hearts. The reactions of partners to threats of infidelity involved intense jealousy and even elaborate display of affection in an attempt to win back the straying partner. Jealousy can lead to violent and selfish behavior; therefore, it is important to understand the most potent triggers.

Jealousy and infidelity are normally interconnected. When you feel that another person is posing a threat to your relationship, jealousy creeps in. Researchers have noted that jealousy has characteristics of fear of loss, anger, and distrust because one is afraid of losing his/her current relationship on account of a rival. Typically, jealousy serves as a means by which a person remains hypervigilant to protect a relationship from unwanted intruders. A common scenario which can result in jealousy is when a partner is in the presence of a threatening person resulting in the sense that he/she might be unfaithful.

There are different theories of infidelity, and every side has an explanation. If we look at social role theorists versus the evolutionary psychologists, there is a difference in how distress is weighed. The evolutionists have focused on forced choice alternatives, whereby the respondents are forced to select the answer they find more upsetting. The choices involve emotional infidelity, whereby a spouse gets emotionally attached to someone else without necessarily getting emotional or physical infidelity which a spouse gets physically intimate with someone without necessarily getting emotionally attached. This paradigm has revealed that men are more upset about physical (sexual infidelity) while women are more likely to get distressed about emotional infidelity.

From the evolutionally perspective, the differences in gender lead to differing reactions to infidelity. This perspective states that women fear that when men get emotionally attached to other women, they will lose the resources they get from men. On the other hand, men fear that women will share the resources with other men who never participated in gathering them. The two genders are more concerned about resources and who they reach. Thus, jealousy arises.

However, not everyone agrees with this theory. Some people feel that the differences in opinions are as a result of the way questions are posed. If people were given a chance to give an opinion rather than chose from just two options, the results might change. However, we can extend on the evolutionary perspective; we might see the true base of argument about jealousy and material possession concern. Jealousy might have risen as a result of resource challenges, whereby a couple might not have enough for their needs and therefore will want to protect the little they have from intruders. In such a case, a male partner may have more concerns about physical infidelity in the event he suspects that the child carried by the woman is not his.

On the other hand, women would be more jealous if they suspect that their hard-earned resources are being diverted to other people instead of their offspring. Consequently, the women will be more jealous if they suspect that the man has developed emotional connections with someone else because there is the risk of resource reallocation.

One needs to identify ways to overcome such disruptive emotions and feelings. First, communication with a partner can help one to clarify any misunderstandings. In case the suspicions are true, the partners will find a way to solve their problem without relying on jealousy and its consequences. Without reliable communication, spouses may have very slim chance of fully comprehending the perspective of each other. If jealousy becomes a seriously pressing issue that completely affects the relationship and its quality, counseling might come in handy. In a counseling setting, the couple can benefit from a professional counselor who will dedicate time to finding a fix for the issues.

Is there good jealousy?

Researches show that a bit of jealousy is healthy for relationships especially when couples are in the initial stages. Trust has not yet developed at the start of a relationship. Therefore, a moderate amount of jealousy can show and fuel commitment. Regulated amounts of jealousy are often considered an expression of attachment, and one can tell if it is safe to invest further in the relationship. When a partner uses jealousy to indicate the importance of faithfulness, the other spouse can be reassured to invest in the relationship.

Chapter 6: The Two Sides of the Affair – the Betrayed and the Cheater

Love is the core of humanity. Intimacy is considered an indicator of love in marriages and romantic relationships. The need for both love and intimacy is hardwired in every human being, be it dreamers, madmen, doers, or the perfectly sane. However, these feelings can also bring us to our lowest moments and even make us feel a breaking emptiness, despair, and sadness. Almost everyone who has experienced love knows how far it can take someone. Probably, the worst part of love is discovering that the person you are in love with is falling for someone else. The thought that someone we are committed to is probably getting intimate with another can make us emotional in unexpected ways.

Infidelity occurs across the world and in many cultures; therefore, you should not despair too much by thinking you are the only person undergoing such a loss. It has been happening for many ages, and it seems classic though we condemn it.

As seen earlier, there are a variety of reasons why people choose to cheat on their spouses. In most cases, an affair is the external break of something wrong on the inside for a while. In some cases, infidelity has nothing to do with the marriage. A person can be happily married and still choose to stray. According to researches, a good number of men and women straying from long-term relationships revealed that their marriages are either happy or very happy. Why do people cheat, then? There is a list of reasons why people stray, be it personality, biological evolution, genetics, et cetera. However, infidelity is always a choice.

The more we understand the causes of cheating, the easier it might be to heal and move on. Understanding the causes can help to draw the line between the acts of infidelity and the forever and ever of the relationship.

In cases of cheating, there is the offender and the offended. If you are the betrayed, know that the infidelity may have nothing to do with you or the relationship. You are not responsible for the actions of your partner, and he/she had the choice to seek better solutions rather than cheating. Having that in mind, it is important to look at a relationship with openness after infidelity. Both the cheater and the cheated on have to look at the ways they might have contributed to the infidelity. Not that anyone has a good enough reason to cheat and neither does anyone deserve to be cheated on, but there are things you might have done that pushed the other away. If your spouse was trying to express loneliness or dissatisfaction, while you were busy ignoring him/her, then you facilitated the cheating. You don't deserve the cheating, but neither did your partner deserve to be pushed aside.

If you have been open, loving, and attentive all along, then the cheating will not make sense to you. However, if you want to continue with the relationship, there is the need to forgive and move forward. Remember, forgiving does not mean forgetting immediately. It also does not mean accepting what happened. Forgiving means understanding enough to stop the anger and hurt form controlling you. People make mistakes, and sometimes, they are really bad. Some of them will put you down for a long while. But know, with the right willpower, you can heal and even continue with the relationship.

If you are the one who strayed and turned your affection to someone other than your spouse, you need to decide whether you want the relationship to go in. Look at the reasons leading you to stray. Take responsibility for your actions, be accountable, be patient, and practice honesty with yourself and with your spouse. Be loving and understanding through the hurt, the anger, the regret, and the intense jealousy until you find a way to solve the issues permanently.

One of the questions that a person (especially the one cheated on) can keep asking him/herself is if the infidelity meant falling out of love. Honestly, anything involving human beings is hardly ever black and white. People have different personalities; thus, life is complicated. The complex nature of human beings can make a good person look like a bad one and vice versa. For instance, a person who cheated because he/she felt deserted can appear like a really bad person while it was the first time. That complexity can make love feel dead for a while such that a person goes to look for the nice feeling outside the relationship.

Most people who have affairs are actually in love with their primary partner, and a good number of people having affairs are not cheaters by nature. If one were completely out of love with the main partner, they would leave rather than have an extra affair. Some off these people in an affair are not liars and betrayers, so we cannot classify them as bad people. True, their deeds are wrong, but everyone is human, capable of making catastrophic mistakes. We all do; we all will.

What I find most interesting is that people being in an affair is not about wanting a different relationship, rather, it is about wanting a difference in the primary relationship. Every marriage and relationship changes with time, and consequently, our needs might get left behind. We can forget things such as connection, love, validation, nurturing, and intimacy as life gets complicated with other tasks. These complications are not a valid reason for people to cheat, but understanding the things that fueled straying can help to fix a relationship.

Cheaters Will Always Be Caught

Cheaters will be caught, be it today, tomorrow, next year or ten years from now. And that will not end well. A cheater does not have to be caught red-handedly with solid proof. No, it could be in a way he/she never imagined–a most minute way, almost too cheap. There are behavior changes that accompany cheating:

- A spouse may start treating his/her partner better or worse.
- A wife may change certain habits; for instance, start working out more. However, this is not always the case.
- A person may start to lie unnecessarily.
- There might be unexplained calls and messages.
- Sudden changes in moods, among others.

There might be legitimate reasons for these behaviors, but if one suspects something is not adding up, an investigation might ease the mind. In the end, a cheater will be caught because that is nature. The changes become too prevalent to hide. Even when the cheater has covered his/her tracks, the other person will get to a point where he/she wants more and more time. Consequently, one will observe more calls and messages without clear explanations. The emotional rift following an affair is very hard to miss. There will be something that will signal the other that something is wrong. Sometimes, the cheater can sell him/herself out by being too careful. Either way, cheating will make life complicated no matter how smart one is.

Normally, a cheater who is caught has cheated more than once. A one-time cheater can get away with his/her actions but will confess one day due to guilt. Someone who cheats often will at one point of the other get too comfortable especially if he/she has done it continuously without being caught. Because of the continuous deceit, the deceived partner may have a hard time forgiving the cheating partner. The offender might not even show remorse for his/her actions since it has become a norm. Too much cheating might render the cheater shameless and guiltless. Without remorse or guilt, the cheater appears not to care about the spouse at all.

If the guilty person, however, confesses because of shame and guilt, it is less likely that he/she has cheated for long. That does not necessarily mean the cheater has not cheated for long, but confession creates a good platform for forgiveness especially if it is accompanied by regret, remorse, and empathy for the innocent partner.

Keep this rule of thumb in mind: A cheater with a conscience, empathy, remorse, and empathy for the partner will regret hurting the relationship thus is more likely to commit to rebuilding what he/she broke. In other words, infidelity does not have to be the end of your relationship, rather, it can be a learning point from a stupid mistake. A good partner will promise never to cheat and keep his/her word.

If you have caught a spouse cheating, and he/she does not feel worried, shocked, remorseful, regretful, sorry for hurting you, or awful because of being caught, you are probably in a wrongful relationship. That person might feel bad for being caught but not for his/her actions. Anyone who shows genuine pain and guilt for being caught and is willing to rectify things in the relationship has a stronger chance of working things out. You will need to do a lot to rebuild the relationship, but the affair can be a thing of the past.

Chapter 7: Tell or Not to Tell?

Marriages and relationships are mostly based on trust and honesty. Most of us demand the truth, the whole truth, and nothing but the truth from our partners. And most of us want to tell the truth to our partners to keep the relationship healthy. But when it comes to infidelity and any act of cheating, should we tell? We often feel torn between telling and not telling because we wonder if it will build or destroy our relationship.

You may already have heard of the phrase *what happens in Vegas stays in Vegas*. The thought behind this saying is to protect a home by ensuring that what happens outside the marriage should not affect the home in any way. As such, your spouse does not need to know anything that might affect them negatively so long as it happened in privacy. However, is this idea good for a relationship where one person has cheated? Does it save or destroy a marriage? I never gave the idea much thought until a friend confided in me that he had had an affair with a stranger some years back while on an office trip. It had never occurred to me that this friend could cheat–I was stunned. He further told me that he never told his wife.

Then, I realized my loss. Should he or should he not tell? So I asked him why he never reported the same to the wife. He explained that he never saw the need or the benefit. After all, the affair ended as soon as he was back home, and he does not have the intention to cheat again. For him, giving such news would only bring sorrow and needless pain to the wife, and she might even decide to revenge. To some extent, I agreed with him. He also explained that, although he feels guilty and sometimes wants to share the same with his wife, he does not do it to release his guilt. For him, the affair happened years ago, and it is not worth risking the family for by telling. He further stated that the marriage has been better since he cheated, and he has put all his effort into building what they have to date.

After the conversation, I did not judge the friend for cheating. After all, he seemed remorseful and would do anything to undo what had happened. However, I could help to put myself in the shoes of the wife. If I were her, would I want to know such a thing or not? Is my husband right and rational by hiding this information?

Considering that marriage is about openness and trust, it would be better if the husband shares what happened with his wife. First, it will lift the weight of guilt from him, and secondly, the wife might get angry, but this openness might bring about a better bond. Who knows, maybe the wife is also dying to share her own experiences.

From a personal perspective and experience, I believe that lying and keeping secrets while in an intimate relationship can do more harm than good. You may choose to keep what happened before you met as a secret, but anything happening while you are in the relationship should be shared. However, I also understand why one may choose to keep things secret for the sake of the relationship and the wellbeing of the partner. Before we proceed with the discussion of whether to tell or not to tell, we should understand what holds a relationship together. A long-term relationship is not glued together by money, sex, or the kids. A long, happy, and healthy relationship is held together by trust. Therefore, when trust is broken, the relationship is violated, even if one chooses to keep the infidelity as secret. Sometimes, keeping a secret is the same as lying. The main focus in infidelity is not the physical or emotional act; it is the loss of trust instead. When you think of it, infidelity does not hurt for the cheated on spouse because of the physical or emotional acts of their partners. Rather, it is the manipulation, the broken trust, the lies of omission and commission, and the fact that everything begins to look different.

Infidelity is something a cheating partner will keep secret until he/she is caught or has to tell. This indicates that infidelity immediately causes guilt, and the cheating spouse knows the risks involved. The cheating spouses who choose to keep their actions under the carpet justify their decisions with the thought that what the partner does not know cannot hurt him/her. Every cheater will engage in some form of justification and denial and will somehow manage to convince themselves that their reasons are right and valid. However, they are wrong what a spouse does not know, especially if its kept secret will hurt the relationship. Even though a betrayed person may not have a clue about the actions of his/her partner, he/she will feel some form and degree of physical or emotional distraction. Sadly, the innocent partner will blame him/herself for the drift in the relationship and even start looking for ways to fix things without understanding the cause. If the innocent partner asks the cheating partner about the perceived rift, the offender might take a defensive and angry stand.

Still, cheaters believe that they are right by keeping secrets. The best and immediate course to take is to lie and be defensive. Agreeably, this tactic will work for a while in the right setting. However, the cheater will not hide forever because he/she is always caught. If you keep getting away with infidelity, well and good, you are doing a good job at lying and faking, and I will not judge you. Be warned though, your relationship is not safe as you imagine. Your partner might be aware of your blatant lies and still opt not to ask. He/she may feel the distance and emotional unavailability and still choose not to ask you. This is not good for your relationship. Getting away with it does not make your partner stupid; however, it makes you more likely to cheat next time an opportunity presents itself. Your relationship will deteriorate further.

To save your partner from unexplained agony, it is better if you come clean. Confession will most likely anger your partner, but it will also save him/her from unexplained self-blame for the rift in the relationship. So, if you value your spouse and what you have built together, ensure that you come clean eventually. At such a point, you have to consider if you are willing to risk everything to save your relationship and even make it better. There is a risk in confession; a spouse might learn about cheating and immediately decide to leave the relationship for good. However, most relationships do not end up dead due to confessions of infidelity. Most of the spouses understand if the cheating partner is remorseful and regretful about their actions. The cheated-on partner will get angry and even accuse the cheating spouse of other things but will always forgive. It will take a lot on the side of the cheating partner to restore the relationship, but so long as the spouses are willing to work together and improve their commitment to each other, there is a huge chance of healing, surviving and even thriving.

The key to rescuing a relationship after infidelity is not keeping secrets. Rather, it is about restoring the broken trust. BE WARNED, broken trust can be hard to mend especially in marriages and intimate relationships, but time is known to heal wounds. Confessing and staying faithful for a while will not automatically repair the relationship trust. Instead, it takes consistency, patience, and painful action of telling the truth and staying accountable. Rebuilding this trust means that you will have to keep telling the truth no matter how painful it is. It does not matter that your partner will get upset if you tell that truth; you have to do it. Staying truthful to the end can be difficult. Both the offender and the offended partners will not enjoy it.

However, with love and respect for the significant other, you will succeed in making the relationship healthy again.

As much as we have looked at reasons why we should be open with our spouses, there are things to consider before opening up:

- If you have a long history of cheating instead of just one of a few isolated cases, seek professional help before making revelations. It is better to seek help from a professional counselor. Even if the partner demands to know everything immediately, one should ensure that he/she holds the information until the right moment. Some information can be too devastating to give out, therefore, take time to decide.

- Consider your safety. Is there a probability that your partner might turn violent when you tell the truth? If you are in the way of physical harm, do not tell.

- There are some experts who suggest that silence is better if the cheating was a one-time mistake. Telling the truth might help you walk away from guilt, but it might hurt your spouse. In some cases, telling a spouse that you cheated changes from having done something hurtful to directly hurting the person. It is worth noting that opening up might help you solve a relationship that was already on the rocks. Telling might help one get past the mistake and even get forgiven, but sometimes, it is best not shared.

- You need to consider your intentions of stopping. Sharing information about infidelity can be very damaging; therefore, you need to understand why you want to tell. If you want to be with your partner and you know very well that telling him/her can lead to the end of the relationship, then do not share. Work with a counselor and look for ways to stay faithful henceforth. Sometimes, there is no value in sharing information about things that will no longer be happening. Avoid passing the pain baton if the other person cannot handle it well even with the help of a counselor. Instead, look for ways to fulfill what you were looking for outside by cheating at home. You could work on your relationship and yourself to be better.

- Has the spouse asked about it? If your spouse has been suspicious and is asking about it, tell the truth. At least your dilemma on how to break the news is now solved. Telling, in this case, will not be a disservice; instead, it will help your partner fill a gap he/she was struggling with all along. It does not mean that he/she will take the news very well, but you will have overcome the biggest hurdle. If the partner already knows about your acts and wants to confirm, then you go ahead and lie straight in their face. There are very slim chances of ever fixing the relationship.

- If you want to break up with your current partner because you have found another lover, then the current one deserves to know the truth. Telling a spouse why you are leaving will not only help him/her move on but also solve a crisis that might have remained if he/she did not understand the events leading to separation.

- If you know that your spouse will find out about your infidelity anyway, be the first to tell. If you still want your relationship, make sure that your spouse hears about your mistakes from you before anyone else. A partner will feel more betrayed if he/she finds out from other people or thorough investigation. Be in the front line to own up your mistake.

- If you cannot break the infidelity habit, end the relationship and be honest about it. If you keep sliding back to cheating even after you promise yourself to stop, be open with your partner. It will help the cheated-on partner to understand the cause of the gap or drift in the relationship and also give closure. If you are not ready or you cannot stay faithful to one partner, let the other person know the truth.

- Get opinion from your partner. Before telling, please ask your spouse what he/she would do in case of infidelity. Some couples would prefer to know while some will prefer to not ever hear about it. From such an understanding, you will know whether or not to tell.

Chapter 8: Vengeance

One of the most devastating discoveries in a relationship or marriage is finding that your partner, a person you trusted and looked to spend the rest of your life together, is cheating. It leaves you hurting, bleeding, and in total anguish. For a colleague of mine called Mike (name withheld), finding that his wife was cheating left him diver stated. He lost count of time, seasons, and meaning of life and was engulfed in the intensity of emotions such as anger, fear, rejection, guilt, and betrayal.

The wife was only on a mission to teach the husband a lesson after discovering that he had been having a series of affairs with different partners. Rebecca chose to retaliate by having an affair. She was beautiful and attractive enough after all. Mike suffered from rejection, abandonment, and neglect when he found out yet for the wife; it was just a simple 'getting even' act.

Infidelity by a spouse or partner evokes a predictable kind of rage in the scorned partner, and it comes with the urge to seek revenge. Whether the spouse chooses to forgive or pursue the matter with revenge depends on internal and external factors. Experts argue that the urge to slash some tires or throw a phone out of a window is deeply instinctual. This means that revenge is primitively impulsive after all. It is more of retaliation aggression intended to protect us from being cheated. Generally, revenge is designed to keep people from taking advantage of you. That is why, when a person punches you, you punch them back. The protective instinct serves as a deterrent, keeping other people from hurting you. However, revenge or vengeance can go awry.

When a person discovers that his/her partner has been cheating, a feeling of scorn develops and some ancient parts of the brain such as the ventral striatum and amygdala react first. The amygdala takes note of the threat, and the ventral striatum combined with nucleus acumens notes how good it would feel about paying back. From there, the more sophisticated region of the brain called the prefrontal cortex, which is responsible for self-control and social behavior, intervenes. If this brain section is not functioning appropriately for one reason or the other such an injury, hunger, lack of sleep, intoxication or any other form of impairment, the person has a harder time resisting the urge to seek vengeance. Research also reveals that in some people, there is less communication between the prefrontal cortex and the other sections of the brain; therefore, we are more likely to revenge.

Surprisingly, researchers found that satisfaction from revenge is more inherent when carried out against a romantic partner. This might be the reason why most people seek to revenge when they realize that their partner has cheated. Although there are no scientific reports on why revenge appears to be sweeter against a sexual partner, experts know that women and men are likely to experience the desire for revenge at similar levels. However, men are more likely to act upon the desired revenge compared to women, and they will inflict harm when revenging. A large portion of home violence is men retaliating—beating their wives in revenge for infidelity, either imagined or real. As such, there is a need for further research on why vengeance seems to feel good in case of infidelity.

Revenge and retaliation cheating is a common choice for most spouses upon discovering that a partner has cheated. Generally, men will resort to domestic violence once they find out that the wife has been in extramarital affairs, and they may choose to leave while women will settle more for retaliation affairs. When a hurt spouse chooses to retaliate, he/she feels justified. Some of these hurt spouses will go to the extent of identifying someone who they know will cause total devastation to the cheating partner. It may be a best friend, a colleague, a business rival, or even a family member. Many of these spouses will make sure that the cheating partner has found out about their deeds even if it means catching them red-handed. The mentality is that the cheating must humiliate the offender as much as it hurt the other person. It is usually about teaching the other person a lesson. However, it is worth noting that retaliation hardly gives the expected results.

Retaliation and revenge are very dangerous, and instead of hurting the guilty partner, they destroy any chances of the recovery of relationships. Instead of the spouses dealing with the problem of infidelity, they end up dealing with multiple issues which complicate the scenario further. The outcome usually is fatal and will leave the spouses hurting ore.

There are several reasons why every spouse should avoid engaging in acts of infidelity with the intention of revenge:

- *Retaliation affairs destroy relationship recovery.*

    When any partner discovers that the spouse has been cheating and engages in a revenge plan, they become distracted from addressing the fundamental cause of cheating. Everyone concentrates on revenging, therefore, ignores the possible ways of addressing the situation comprehensively. When a relationship has already been affected by an affair, it is vulnerable. Therefore, revenge and retaliation will only complicate things further. Consequently, there will be further mistrust as a result of betrayal and deception, and the couples will drift further apart. Simply put, retaliation is adding fuel to an already burning fire.

- *Retaliation and revenge will stall your recovery.*

  Discovering that a partner has been cheating often leaves one feeling violated, rejected, and violated. Retaliation might seem like a good solution, but it is not a real cure. Revenge will only accelerate the feelings of rejection and disrespect with emotions of guilt and pain for making the partner feel more devastation. At this juncture, it is important for every person to face his/her individual feelings on a personal level or with the help of a therapist. Choosing to revenge instead of dealing with the pain is choosing to stay in denial, and this will only delay the healing process.

- *Retaliation with infidelity only dents your image.*

  Taking everything into account, retaliation affairs are childish and only offer a coping mechanism, which is generally retrogressive and benefits only you. Revenge is merely a way of acting out and getting back to your partner, showing signs of childishness. It reflects a lot of immaturities and does not do one any good instead; it destroys the foundations of the relationship you have built over time.

- *Retaliation will only suck you into a blame game.*

  Normally, the cheating partner will turn the blame on the innocent spouse when caught. It can be something like, you no longer groom well, you are too busy to meet my needs, you are no longer attractive and approachable, or any other reason they find valid. Retaliating by infidelity will only give the offender another reason to blame you. In the mind of the cheating partner, you are already to blame, why then should you add him/her another reason to blame you?

Whatever you choose to do, retaliation will never work. The best revenge is to achieve success. Make sure that you win in whatever you desire. Try to solve the crises, and at the same time, make sure you are succeeding in whatever you do. You deserve to thrive and win.

True, we are hard-wired to want revenge when we are wrong, but as seen earlier, vengeance against a cheating partner does not benefit you. If anything, it keeps you from healing your wounds. So it is important that we stop our vengeful thoughts in their tracks before they turn into regrettable actions. Our chances of healing will be higher if we stop the desire to play tit for tat.

How do you channel your revenge energy?

1. *Do well.* As the old saying goes, doing well is the best revenge. Focus all your energy to being a better person. In fact, strive to be such a good person that the cheating partner feels the loss. You will not only heal faster and feel better about yourself, but also will be an inspiration to everyone who knows what is happening behind the scenes. Mature responses are more likely to win in such a case. Remember that cheating spouses are known to pass the blame to the innocent partners. Seek to fulfill your own goals, create your happiness, and be better. Learning how to play the piano and getting back to shape will give you more satisfaction than imagining how you will clean out the toilet bowl with the toothbrush of the offender.

2. *Create.* In the moment of feeling betrayed, cheated, and probably scorned, your first intention should be to divert

the need for revenge. You need to identify ways to get rid of the story that's taking the front seat and blackening your heart. This can be accomplished by allowing yourself to feel the hurt and betrayal then diverting that energy into creating. Look for an activity that can preoccupy your mind and body such as cooking, writing, drawing, or building. Creativity is a healing force, and when one engages in it, the mind becomes free from the immediate pain.

3. *You are in charge.* The spouse who cheated on you does not have any control over your feelings. You are the only one with enough power to allow him/her to control you. Otherwise, you are in charge of your words, thoughts, and actions. Once you recognize that, it is hard for the offenders to run you. It becomes easier to stick to the ideas you hold dear such as nonviolence and forgiveness. Through understanding that you are in charge of yourself will empower you to stay within your boundaries. Whenever you find yourself thinking of the pain you feel and a way to revenge, divert your thoughts to something positive. Remember, you are in charge.

4. *Choose to forgive.* The truth is, infidelity is emotionally devastating for most people. It will not be easy to forgive someone who betrayed your trust, neither will it be easy to overcome the excruciating pain of infidelity. However, you can easily move towards that point and overcome the desire to revenge. You do not have to push towards reconciliation, neither do you have to forget the hurtful action. But you have to recognize that your spouse is a human being, and he/she made a bad choice without deep consideration. That way, you will have allowed yourself to move towards a brighter side of life. Revenge might have such devastating consequences. In fact, you might end up

in court or jail for having destroyed his/her property. Taking such consequences into account, it is better if you walk away from vengeance and let it go.

Chapter 9: Is Sex Just Sex?

According to the philosophy of romanticism, sex is not just sex. It is a sign of committing to someone wholly. This mentality has made it hard for people to forgive their partners when they find out about cheating, especially sexually. When we look at infidelity as just sex, it can be easier to forgive and let go. However, researches insist that cheating is not about sex. There is a myriad of reasons why people engage in acts of infidelity.

It is not surprising that when a person is caught cheating, there are a lot of stories based on truths and lies. Culture has taught us that a romantic partner is there to meet the needs of their spouse be it love, security, or comfort. As such, we are quick to judge and lay blame when a person is caught with a case of infidelity. We lay blame on the perpetrator and assume that they have gone against the norms of relationships out of a personal will. The person cheating is seen as the betrayer of trust.

However, although we choose to lay the blame on the offender (the person cheating) entirely, assuming that they are selfish people who want to have their cake and eat it too, the reality is more striking. There are countless reasons as to why a partner may choose to cheat, and when analyzed closely, then we realize that sex is not just sex.

Infidelity is not just about sexual involvement with a person. The reasons for cheating mentioned in the previous chapter indicate that there is more to infidelity than sex. Very few couples cheat for the sake of sex or sexual satisfaction. Regardless of the stereotypic belief, majority of infidelity does not occur because of bedroom boredom. The most commonly cited reason for infidelity is emotional distance. Although sex plays a role in building emotional intimacy, a large extent of commitment is created with the lights on.

Emotional connection is created through small connection moments such as a good morning kiss, a secret smile before a meeting, a sweet message at work, and sharing how the day was in the evening. These simple things let a spouse know that he/she is cared for and loved. When these unconscious reassurances of love vanish, a partner might cheat to get the feeling. Some people may engage in sex for the sake of sex, and normally, such people have less restrictive views about limiting a person to one sexual partner. Researchers have found that a person is likely to cheat if he/she has cheated before.

A study conducted in the United Kingdom among 5,000 people revealed that men and women have a variety of reasons for cheating. The top five reasons cited by women included lack of emotional intimacy, failed communication between the partners, tiredness, had sex history, and loss of interest in the current partner. For men, lack of communication leads the list, followed by stress, sexual dysfunction with the spouse, lack of emotional intimacy and fatigue. These reasons can prove that sex in infidelity cases id not just sex.
If we have a hard time genuinely communicating with our partners or we do not feel valued in our current relationships, chances of straying are high. People need to invest energy and time into their relationships or infidelity will take over otherwise. There is also the need to understand the right way of investing time and energy in a relationship. Keep checking with your partner if you are doing what it takes to build a healthy relationship. Are your actions and choices good enough for him/her?

While some couples might engage in infidelity due to an excessive desire for sex, most people cheat for reasons they can solve or work on with their partners. If you are having a hard time sorting out your relationship because your spouse or partner cheated, seek professional help.

It does not matter if a cheating spouse cheated for the sake of sex or to fulfill some other need; the consequences are devastating. The cheating partner losses interest in the marriage or relationship, while the cheated-on partner feels hurt, devastated, and scorned. The offender might feel at a loss for being found out and can identify all excuses and reasons for cheating, while the faithful spouse has to face hurt, uncertainty, rejection, and betrayal. The worst part is that the cheating partner might not be willing to admit that he/she did a hurtful thing. Maybe it would be easier to recover from infidelity if affairs were just about sex, but the realization that there are other underlying reasons for cheating leaves us unsure and questioning.

Once the emotional part of infidelity is involved besides sex, cheating becomes complicated. Emotional affairs can lack sexual elements, whereby a person has a secret emotional bond with a person who is not their spouse. Emotional infidelity involves having someone else become the primary source of emotional gratification. Gradually, this secret partner becomes more important to the cheating person than the spouse.

Consequently, the emotional intimacy in the relationship and marriage becomes drained, and hearts get pulled apart. In all forms of cheating, an offender feels some needs are missing in the primary relationship. They use any excuse available to break their vows and promises. Rationalization is easy for most cheaters, but it is even easier for people having an emotional affair because they can defend themselves by saying that there is no physical connection. What they fail to realize is that infidelity is worse when emotions are involved. Although sexual infidelity hurts and sex can be assumed as just sex, emotional infidelity is very strenuous to a relationship.

A relationship should be respected and valued to avoid all forms of infidelity. Cheating is not just cheating, sex is not just sex, and emotional infidelity is not just friendship. However, if you can look at sex as just sex, ensure that your spouse shares the same opinion before engaging other sexual partners. If our partner prefers monogamy and exclusivity, respect that and look for a way to come to a consensus.

Chapter 10: After the Affair

There is nothing simple about finding out that a spouse has been cheating—it is heartrending. For most people, it is a place where they never thought they would find themselves. The trust given by spouses in a relationship makes it hard to imagine that a person may cheat or get cheated on. Infidelity is a pain that couples are rarely prepared for. Therefore, they have a hard time moving on after the affair. In this era, there are a lot of issues that may lead a couple down the road of infidelity, including social media temptation, financial stress, parenting stress, work and home imbalances, pornography, et cetera.

Arnold and Gloria were the couples to look up to when it came to the most excellent relationships. They had been together since college and had held a perfect wedding immediately after school. Soon after, the couple added two babies to the family and life seemed to be moving well and fast. However, Arnold discovered that he had failed one paper which was necessary to proceed on with a course he was taking. He was devastated. Gloria offered to support him as he went for study and retake. The paper took a lot of time and energy from Arnold, but Gloria offers all she could see so that Arnold could pass. After a while, Gloria noticed some weird behavior in Arnold. He was taking calls at very odd hours and would talk for long.

Additionally, the study sessions increased and extended until late at night. That did not alarm Gloria as much as the emotional and physical rift she started experiencing. Arnold seemed withdrawn, and he did not participate in dinner talks which they held often. Gloria thought that maybe she had failed to meet certain needs and whenever she asked, Arnold blamed the weight of the forthcoming exam.

Gloria started fearing that her husband had met another woman who was preoccupying his thoughts. Those fears came true when she found out that Arnold had been going out with a female medical student and was finding emotional and physical comfort in her. Gloria did not know what to do because her marriage was still very young and nothing had prepared her for such situations. All she could do was pray and seek guidance from friends. How was she going to fight for her marriage?

Finding out that a spouse you once trusted with your life has an affair can cause intense and deep emotional pain. If you have gone through it or are going through this discovery currently, my heart goes out to you. The sting of deception, loss of trust, and sense of betrayal can be very overwhelming. Normally, infidelity triggers deep emotions in both the offender and the innocent spouse. The emotions felt due to physical infidelity can be as intense as those felt in an emotional affair. No matter the type of infidelity, trust is broken and the impact can be devastating.

Once a person discovers that his/her partner has engaged in an affair, a lot of questions arise. The innocent spouse can start to question the trueness of the marriage or relationship. He or she will try to identify his/her mistakes in the marriage–where could he/she have failed? Typically, the spouses will discover that one person or both have been struggling with issues such as self-esteem, substance abuse, alcoholism, or things from the past such as sexual abuse or trauma. They might also discover that some marital problems have been brewing over the years but they never really sorted them out. These unspoken matters will have caused silence, disconnection, and gradual separation of the hearts. In the cases where the marriage is a happy one and still a spouse opts to cheat, chances are the person is missing certain things in his/her own life and is looking to discover or rediscover them. However, affairs are not the answer to any marital challenges or concerns. Typically, an affair is born out of fantasy as one seeks to escape reality, either personal or marital. And the external person is seen as the temporal cure to the challenges.

If you are in a situation such as Arnold and Gloria's, do not call it quits yet. The first defense after finding out about an affair is the mentality of quitting. The anger and feeling of loss of trust make one question if he/she will ever be able to work with the spouse on the relationship ever again. Do not be in a rush to end what you have probably worked on for years. Take some time to understand the cause of the straying and seek professional help if need be. It might take a lot of hard to open up and listen to a spouse and even trust his/her word after such a situation, but patience might show the two of you where a step was missed. During the analysis of the situation, you will need to give each other time and space. Some therapists may even recommend temporary separation. The deep emotions of grief and betrayal coming from the discovery of an affair might lead one to do or say things they would not have, therefore the need for space.

Infidelity may look different for every couple. Each one should look for a counselor to help them with guidance suited for the situation. We should also understand that both the offender and the offended suffer after the discovery. The cheater may suffer from guilt, denial, low self-esteem, shame, difficulties facing the family, et cetera. The offended may struggle with distress, shame, hurt, rejection, et cetera.

This paragraph addresses the two spouses, the guilty and the innocent.

You will feel overwhelmed by the amount of emotion you are undergoing. These emotions may be anything from intense sadness to utter devastation and any feelings in between. Some moments you will feel guilt, while others you will want to take the defensive side. I can guarantee you that some days, it will be hard to get out of bed and pursue your goals. However, all that depends on the amount of trust you had in each other.

To function well during these moments of heart-wrecking feelings, you will need to take great care of yourself to avoid falling into depression and other states of helplessness. Ensure that you meet your basic needs– eat, sleep, exercise–and engage in healthy stress management practices. Although it can be difficult than normal and may sound impossible, the more you eat sleep and practice healthy living, the better you will be placed to think clearly.

As you try to understand what happened, you will realize that there are a lot of questions popping up in your mind, the whys, hows, your value, the details of the affair, how it started and why, the true character of your spouse, and your fault in the equation. Allow yourself to ask all the questions and receive answers you were probably unprepared for even when it hurts. Complete honesty requires strength. Be prepared to give and take in the truth, no matter how harsh it is. Be prepared to question our worth and the worth of your relationship. Infidelity leads to a battlefield which requires strength.

Seek support from family and friends. During this time, you will be tempted to think that you are the only one who has undergone such difficulties and thus lack the courage to share. You might also be tempted to look at the relationships that failed after such an experience. Isolation and loneliness will seem like a good option. However, sharing will help you realize that a lot of people have undergone what you are experiencing and even worse. Look for reliable and positive support. Seek help from those who can give you unbiased advice.

Pay attention to your heart. It may take time to heal because you will have to forgive your spouse for feeling peaceful again. Note that, forgiving does not mean forgetting. And it does not mean that you have to make up with your partner. Forgiving means giving yourself peace by letting go of the pain. Forgiving benefits you more than anyone else, so take the step.

Look to understand your contributions to the challenges in your marriage. How did you facilitate your spouse to cheat or how could you have solved the matters instead of having an affair? Although you may want to point fingers at your spouse, there is the need to look at self. *What did I do or fail?* True, you are not responsible for the choices of your partner, but looking at your faults might help you heal and even make your relationships better.

While undergoing all the pain, some of these suggestions might sound ridiculous and impossible. For instance, eating and sleeping might become a problem. Take courage and be patient. You will identify a solution to your challenges.

For the one who cheated, you might ask yourself, how did I get here? You might find yourself regretting and realizing that you did not see it coming. Maybe you intended to find relief without hurting anyone. Regardless of why you chose to stray, there will come the point when you have to face your actions and their consequences. This wake-up call comes with a lot of varying emotions such as regret, remorse, anger, denial, and more. It will even be harder if your spouse chooses to leave while your intention was not to break the relationship. If you are coming out of an affair, you will have to decide whether you want your relationship to continue or you just want to end it. Normally, when one chooses to end the relationship, it is not because of the affair but because of a series of downsides of the relationship which might have accumulated over time.

If you were the one in the affair and you wish to fight for the relationship, this is for you.

A day comes when you have to look at what you did and caused. Not only for you but also your spouse, marriage, and children, if any. When your spouse pieces the lies and deception together, he/she will confront you. It might happen when you least expect. After your race into a fantasy world, you will have to face reality, and chances are you will hit an all-time low. You will have to approach your spouse with enormous brokenness and humility, pleading with him/her for at least a chance to save your marriage/relationship. It will not be easy especially if your spouse is still bitter for being deceived.

If you valued your spouse and had the drama of making a forever home, your heart will be broken with remorse as you look for the opportunity to repair what you broke. Some steps you should consider taking after being unfaithful include:

1. Ending the affair.

    For the sake of your marriage and relationship, stop all contact with the person you were cheating with– messaging, calls, face to face meetings, romantic relations, et cetera. If the other person does not want to let go, ensure that you inform your spouse before he/she gets suspicious. Tell the truth before you are asked. Total honesty will be the beginning of rebuilding your trust and marriage.

2. Take total responsibility for the affair.

    Even though your spouse might have fueled the infidelity, you need to take full responsibility for your actions. Do not pass blame while you are trying to recover your marriage. You betrayed your marriage, spouse, and vows regardless of the issue at hand. It will be very easy and appealing to slide to the blame game but know your mission, make your choices, and set the excuses aside.

3. Understand and empathize with your spouse.

Your partner will have all sorts of emotional responses to your infidelity. Unfaithfulness can make someone doubt everything and react in unpredictable ways. You might feel like your spouse is not seeing the effort you are putting to repair what you broke. Take time to empathize with him/her and understand what it might be like to be cheated on. This is a period of healing and not a time to force your spouse to accept his/her mistakes. Seek to show commitment and fidelity to our relationship. Empathy can help you to understand your partner and even seek heartfelt pardon from him/her.

Therapists say that the first indicator of whether a relationship will survive or not is the ability of the offender to show empathy towards the hurt spouse and feel sorry for the pain caused. You will want to fight back or defend yourself, but for now, do everything you can to empathize and be available for your partner. Answer the questions with honesty. Try to validate the pain felt by your spouse by showing tenderness and compassion. Understand that the pain felt by him/her was caused by you. It will not be easy for either of you thus give each other time to heal and process all the deep emotions.

4. Recommit to your spouse.

   After an affair, there is a need for the offender to express commitment. This can be done through open expression to show the other person that you are all in and are willing to fight for the relationship. Keep in mind that the level of trust in your spouse has been deeply scarred. It might even be lost entirely. Therefore, rebuilding will take effort, time, and commitment. Be very proactive in rebuilding trust.

5. Transparency and honesty must be implemented.

   Your spouse will ask you questions which answers might be very tough on them. However, you have to be honest and transparent since it is the only way to rebuild trust. Tell the entire truth about the affair, its initiation, happening, and ending. Your spouse desperately needs to know the timeframe of the affair so that he/she can piece it together. Ensure that your partner is confident about your text messages, calls, social media communications, friends, whereabouts, et cetera. Be ready to answer serious questions about your day-to-day life for a while. Before your spouse can trust you again, he/she will ask about every detail of your life.

6. Avoid painting too many sexual details for your partner.

   Although honesty is required to rebuild the relationship, avoid telling your spouse about the physical and sexual encounters in details for it will only be traumatizing and hurtful. Even if he/she insists on knowing, engage a counselor to guide you on how and what to tell. Some information might not be useful.

7. Heal your own heart and seek the help you need.

   Even though your attention should be on empathizing with your spouse, you also need help. Just because you are the offender does not mean that you feel nothing. Enormous amounts of emotions such as guilt, shame, unworthiness, et cetera, might be overwhelming you. Your spouse might not be in a position to help you because he/she is dealing with the whole situation. The only way you will make your relationship healthy again is by ensuring that your own heart is healed.

8. Be grateful to your partner.

   He/she has chosen to fight for the relationship even though you made bad choices. That is a real act of sacrifice and love. Ensure that your spouse knows how grateful you are for giving you another chance. Be warned, the shockwaves of cheating will be felt in your relationship and marriage years after the actual incident. However, it is possible to rebuild a relationship that is good or even better than before. Those who have walked down this road will tell you that it is a difficult walk, but the results are worth waiting.

Chapter 11: Become Sexual Again

Erotic recovery is very basic after a case of infidelity. Sex is a very basic part of a relationship, and every couple has to be intimately and erotically connected. Changing from the state of utter disconnect (emotionally and sexually) after an affair may seem difficult and even impossible to some extent more so if you are still in pain. However, if you decide to stay together, it will be necessary that you work together on your sex life. That is a vital part of your healing process.

Erotic recovery will encompass all your vitals, physically, emotionally, and psychologically. Intimacy will have to be considered thoroughly. Until you can move past the erotic difficulties of your relationship, the other person in the relationship will be in bed with you mentally. The bridge between the two of you may seem too wide, but at times, you will crave to be held again. Sex can be a way of recovering and feeling grounded a reminder of what life was like before the infidelity. Couples may find that the things they cannot share through words can be expressed through touch.

At the same time, infidelity can make you build walls so high to guard against any form of vulnerability. It will take time to make love the way you used to but be patient. Do not pressure each other if you are not ready. It is normal to worry about each other after an affair and wonder how the sex life will be.

At times, you will worry that the amount of sex you are having is not enough, while during other moments, you will feel like you are trying too hard. You should check if it is a genuine sex or you are just trying to manipulate your spouse. Talk to your spouse directly about your feelings. Make sure that you communicate about the readiness of having sex. If you are not ready, say it out loud.

There are things you need to know about sex life after a case of infidelity:

1. Sex is an entirely different experience after infidelity. If a couple chooses to move on together after one of them has had an affair, it is a very major step. Recovering together is not an easy process, and this period will test every aspect of the relationship, including sex life. Getting back to the bedroom can be an effective way for a couple to rebuild their trust. However, sex can trigger a series of emotions, and the spouses need to be prepared for the harsh realities surrounding the post-affair relationship.

2. You will not have the same relationship you had before. As you try to move on following an affair, you need to recognize that your past relationship is gone, and it is not coming back. Right now, you have to focus on building the new relationship, and that also includes sex. Do not assume that you will get back to the place you were. The sexual relation you had initially will have gone.

3. You have to be patient until trust comes back. Sex is an incredibly intimate part of a relationship, and emotions run high. If you are still in the stages of recovery where emotions are highly unstable such that you cannot be around each other without getting angry, then you need to take it slow. Let the pressure reduce before you can rush back to the bedroom.

4. In the right time and setting, sex can be a great source of healing. Sex can transport a couple emotionally and physically to places where words cannot go. At the right

time, sex and spending intimate time together can help you restore the bond with your partner.

5. You will have to reprioritize your sex life consciously. Previously, sex was not something that needed a lot of force. It might not have been the best sometime before the infidelity happened, but you did not require thinking, rethinking, and prioritizing. However, you will have to make time for sex during the recovery period consciously. Remember that sex can be a healing experience when you are recovering from an affair. As such, you have to be ready for it, get good at initiating the action and make sex a priority. Get a little adventurous in the bedroom if need be. You will need to show each other the role sex is going to play in your new relationship.

6. You will have to put everything on the table, including the taboo subjects. It will not be easy, but choosing to move on means repairing every aspect of the relationship. You will have to talk about some of the sexual behaviors that lead to the affair. If sex were not amazing anymore, you would have to say it and look for solutions. Address whatever it is that lead to a breach of trust. Do your best to understand the cause of the affair. It will be difficult to open up at first due to the fear of hurting each other, but you will have to do it. You will also have to talk about what happened sexually during the affair. Total honesty is very important for trust.

7. Look out for dysfunctions. Did you know that several people experience sexual dysfunctions after an affair? If it happens in your relationship, do not panic. Some women will have a hard time getting aroused after an affair, while men might fail to get an erection. These things happen mostly in the period of stress and turmoil. Therefore, you

should not panic. Be patient with each other and understand the challenges you might be facing. If you encounter performance problems or if any sexual contact brings about bad memories of the affair, you might have to slow down and take some more time to heal.

Restoring the Intimacy

In some cases, the betrayed spouses will want to heal from the affair through having more sex. He/she might become what some therapists call super sex god/goddess. When the hurting spouse opts for such sex, it becomes great but not necessarily a good thing. The motivation is pain, and the betrayed partner is busy comparing and competing with the third party. There are some things you can do to recover sexually:

1. Do not compare yourself with the affair partner.

   Everyone is unique, so comparing ourselves to others is wrong on all levels. We are like flowers or colors; each one is beautiful, different, and unique. To say that one color is better than another is to err. Beauty is made of diversity. If we said that blue is prettier than red, then did away with the color. The world would be at a complete loss. One can find strengths and weaknesses in everything. There are bad and good things for everyone. Therefore, trying to validate yourself by finding weaknesses in others and vice versa can lead to failure. There is always someone better, smarter, funnier, sexier, more talented, et cetera. Although the super sex resulting from feelings of competition and jealousy is awesome, it will have to move from selfish to the basis of trust, love, and security in the relationship. It will have to be about understanding that you are loved and desired by your partner.

Great sex will have to be about yourself and not the competition. If you stay stuck in self-centered sex, it will lead to failure in the long term. Again, comparison might lead to repulsion. The betrayed partner may hate the idea of the spouse having sex with someone else so much that he/she does not want anything to do with intimacy. The spouse might be willing to forgive, but whenever the thought of sex comes up, interest is lost.

2. Get beyond the feelings of shame, guilt, and unworthiness.

Sometimes, failure to restore sexual intimacy might come from the person who cheated. As indicated above, the person might suffer from too much guilt and shame that he/she is unable to get intimate completely. Some may still find sex hard because they have not ended the affair completely, and they are lost on whether to go on or leave. Surprisingly, some people miss the person they cheated with thus have a hard time engaging the primary partner. This is normal, and it might take some time before the partners get deeply sexual again. There is a lot of grieve and loss taking place at these junctures; therefore, both spouses need to get beyond the affair drama. When a cheating spouse grieves the loss of the other partner, it is not about the person but rather the feeling they had in the affair. During the affair, an unfaithful spouse thinks that he/she is in love, and truly, he/she is in awe because of the way the affair feels. The thought of being loved and cherished by a third party appeals to the person. Intimacy issues are not easy to sort after an affair, and they can be as complex as life. Do not look for a cookie cutter solution.

3. After an affair, restoring the relationship is about 'we', not them/him/her.

   A majority of people, especially the betrayed ones will want to pass the blame. They will think that the offender must restore the relationship. The spouse who cheated may also think that since the other person had failed in one way or the other, it is up to him/her to repair the holes. A couple should realize that it is about the two of them and not just the husband or the wife. They should avoid statements like "he has an issue" or "she is the problem." Intimacy is about two people; healing should be a 'we' thing.

   Spouses should understand the purpose of sex and intimacy in mending a relationship after infidelity. It includes healing, reconciling after an argument, comforting each other, building self-esteem, expressing love in a deeper and more profound way when words fail, reconnecting on a higher level, pleasing each other, and feeling attractive.

4. Do not force things.

   After an affair, sexual intimacy helps the two spouses to heal; the sooner it happens, the better. However, no one should force the other the need for sex may be there but do not overstep or violate each other. Some therapists will say that a couple should wait longer before getting intimate, but it is crucial for the two people to connect as soon as possible.

5. Do not take sexual intimacy as a sign of full reconciliation.

    Although sexual intimacy is part of the reconciliation process, the spouses, (especially the offender) should not assume that all is well. A lot of things need to take place before the couple can heal fully. True reconciliation takes time, openness, dedication, and a lot of other virtues. Also note that full reconciliation might be hard if the couple puts sex off for longer than necessary. Some people will not be able to engage without sex, but it is also important to understand that sex does not mean that everything is back to normal.

6. Learn how to converse honestly and openly about with your spouse.

    A couple needs to understand ways of discussing sex openly without judging each other. Opening up about each secret desire and learn the opinion of your spouse is fine. However, avoid talking about intimacy issues during intimacy. Choose a time to talk about it. If you get sexually intimate and things do not go as expected, for instance, one person has a dysfunction, do not feel pressured. Hold each other and wait till the tension dies. Avoid talking about what happened at the moment and wait for a better time to engage one another in the conversation. Simply put, separate moments of sex with the times you have sex talks.

7. Focus on calming lovemaking sex while recovering from infidelity.

    Normally, there are two types of sex: wild, adventurous erotica and lovemaking sex. The two are perfectly fine in a relationship and marriage. However, the recovery period calls for comforting sex. While you focus on rebuilding love and trust, sex should be lovemaking.

8. Heal the broken hearts to heal the intimacy.

Restoring sexual intimacy after a case of cheating requires gentleness, patience, and understanding. You have to know, however, that sexual therapy cannot happen without marriage therapy. The two therapies have to work together. In every relationship and marriage, couples should mirror each other. The content of your marriage will be seen in bedroom affairs and vice versa. As such, you have to heal hearts to achieve the right sexual intimacy.

9. Be willing to fulfill the fantasies of your spouses (within limits).

If a spouse cheated because he/she felt unsatisfied in the relationship, you need to understand the needs met in the affair and be willing to work on them. In rebuilding the relationship, the person who strayed needs to be sensitive to the needs of the betrayed partner in restoring the assurance that they are sexually attractive. When a person does certain things in the affair, he/she should be willing to do them in the primary relationship so long as the betrayed spouse is willing and desires it. A good example of a thing that might happen in a relationship is having sex in a car. The spouses should be willing to try that in the marriage. The bed might be very comfortable but if a spouse wants the adventure of the car, then be willing to try.

Remember that love is an action, and it is not about you only. So, if you are the one who cheated, and you tried something in the affair that you are not willing to in the marriage, then you have a problem that needs to be addressed. You need to ask yourself what the problem is. It could be guilt, depression, shame, or any other thing. Could it be the way your spouse kisses or his/her hygiene? Be open, honest, and have the dissuasion. One thing you can be sure of is that a marriage without intimacy is doomed to fail. As such, any struggles with infidelity should be addressed as soon as possible.

Chapter 12: The Man and Woman Difference

There is the thought that if a woman cheats, she is signaling the end of her primary relationship, unlike a man. A woman cheats for different reasons compared to men, and the previously mentioned idea holds a lot of weight. Men and women see relationships and sex differently. For men, it is easy to segment love and sex. For them, intimate connections and sex are different things. It is more like sex is sex and relationships are relationships. The two hardly overlap. Consequently, a man will cheat casually without easily feeling a degree of emotion, although it is not always the case. On the other hand, a woman will cheat differently where sex and intimacy are tangled, so compatibilization is more difficult.

Easily put, when a woman cheats, there is a degree of intimacy, romance, connection, or love. For men, cheating can be simply a way of fulfilling sexual urges and fantasies that are not met in the primary relationship. Of course, a good number of men cheat both emotionally and sexually because they are attracted to the outside partner, but many more do not. Infidelity for men can be just an opportunistic and primarily sexual activity that does not affect the main relationship. A large number of men will report that they are happy in their primary relationship though they are cheating. Despite cheating, most men who have an affair have no intention of putting their primary relationship to an end.

Women, on the other hand, are less likely to separate love and sex. For the majority of women, sex and a bit of relational intimacy have to go together. More often than not, the intimacy relation is more important than sex for women. That is why women are less likely to cheat unless they feel unhappy in their primary relationship or they are intimately connected with the partner they are cheating with outside. Either of the two reasons can make a woman leave the primary relationship.

A search was conducted where women and men were shown videos of people having sex—two men having sex, two women having sex, and a man-woman sex. Most men were turned on by the video of a man and a woman and also woman-to-woman. Gay men were turned on only by the man-to-man sex. On the other hand, two-thirds of women were turned on by videos where there was an emotional and psychological connection regardless of the gender or sex type. Numerous researches have revealed that, generally speaking, women are turned on by and attracted to emotional intimacy rather than physical intimacy. On the other hand, men are turned on by sex acts whether or not there are committed relationships.

Male sexual desire is driven by physiological factors more than psychological ones. That explains why porn sites designed for men focus so much on overt sexual acts and body parts without adding many hints of emotions. Even porn literature designed for men focuses on sexual acts and not relationships and feelings.

When you tune in on shows and books written for women, you will see that the attention is on the flow of romance, love, relationship, and a happy ever after. You will find very little non-relational and objectified sex in the shows designed for female consumers. Instead, you will see more of love-at-first-sight, hearts melting, a story of two people in a long-term commitment, and heroes. Think of the *Fifty Shades of Grey* movie where the bad boy meets the good girl.

Typically, men do not need love to enjoy sex. They hardly need to like the person; all they want is a turn on, and they are good to go. It is harder to convince a woman to have sex because she will want a considerate man, who wants to have a home and children, and has a sense of humor, is caring and sweet, and a lot of other stuff.

Some researchers and therapists say that the complication in women when it comes to relationships is a result of years of experience. Let's take a look at this: when a woman is considering having sex with a man, the subconscious mind is looking at the long-term results. In the unconscious human software, the woman is aware that sex can alter her life forever. The possible results include pregnancy, nursing, and a life to raise children. Such a commitment would require resources, time, and enormous amounts of energy. As such, any sex with the wrong guy can have devastating results.

Consequently, the woman tends to vet a possible mating partner thoroughly before any physical and psychological engagement or even getting intimate. Women have a safety mechanism hardwired in their mind, and it will not give in to sex until certain conditions are met. Surprisingly, women with histories of sexual trauma will have a weaker self-defense mechanism, and consequently, they are more likely to cheat and get victimized as adults.

Men face fewer dangers when engaging in sex. Therefore, they have not identified the need to guard themselves and develop an inner detector. That is why men are likely to cheat even when they are in a happy relationship. If you were wondering why a relationship where a man cheated is more likely to survive than a woman, it is because when a woman cheats, it takes emotional, physical, and mental energy, while a man can easily engage only the body. A woman will hardly cheat while in a good relationship yet a man will cheat while in a relationship worth dying for easily. Because women are more likely to cheat only when in broken relationships which are not worth saving, there is rarely the need to struggle to rebuild the intimacy, trust, and long-term harmony.

Another interesting fact about infidelity is that men reported feeling worse when they are cheated on sexually. However, women reported more guilt when they cheated emotionally more than physically. The main reason is that women consider emotions a large part of a relationship. Again, men will feel worse about their spouse cheating physically because, for them, sex is a big part of a relationship.

For men, whether they feel guilty or not vary. Some will feel guilty and even want to fight for the primary relationship, others will not. Some therapists say that, although a person may fail to show remorse or guilt of the outside, every cheater feels guilty on the inside to some extent. A cheater who cheats often might acquire the ability to separate him/herself from conscious and feelings. Men especially will become better at compartmentalizing their behavior, believing that the affair has nothing to do with the relationship. Others will justify their acts to keep doing what they do even when they know it's wrong.

Regardless of gender, all cheaters have a conscience. Majority of them did not even set out to cheat, but the habit develops out of a bad decision. Before a person gets back to his/her ordinary self, another bad decision makes them cross the line. It becomes easier to cheat, justify, and enjoy the ride. A cheater will find it more fun to deny than to face the mistakes he/she had done.

Again, regardless of gender, the cheated-on person will feel angry, betrayed, and incredibly hurt. The feelings are understandable and normal. It is important to recognize that, although your feelings are different from those of your partner after cheating, it does not mean that he/she does not have an opinion about the scenario. If he/she is showing none, then it is just hiding. Most cheaters live with their deeds by explaining away their behavior and burying their feelings. Keep in mind that a person who cheats is not necessarily a bad person; he/she has probably just made a bad decision. If you have been cheated on, you need to know that cheaters also feel bad about their choices. Either way, you will have to decide whether to leave or stay in the relationship.

Chapter 13: Rebuilding Trust

Infidelity involves the direct breaking of trust. The immoral act which you cannot share with a spouse because you know it would hurt him/her is breakage.

For a couple to heal a relationship after infidelity, they have to learn ways to tell the truth (more so the cheater) actively. If there is something one person wants to know, the other should be willing to open up and tell the truth. The offender should aim always to volunteer valuable information as soon as possible. The betrayed spouse is already angry because of the infidelity, but he/she will be angrier if the partner keeps secrets. Even a little thing that looks suspicious might bring about emotions and denial.

Unfortunately, the offender might mess up rigorously during the healing process in numerous ways even though he/she is willing to work on the relationship. Some of the pitfalls can involve:

- *Passive truth-telling*. Passive truth-telling will force the betrayed partner to handle all the hard and investigative work. If the betrayed partner feels suspicious that the spouse has done something wrong, he/she must ask. The offender might answer the question but fail to offer other valuable information. However, the betrayed partner might have some of the missing information and will tell when he/she is fed half-truths. A cheater will sometimes try to convince him/herself that he/she is no longer cheating because he/she is not lying or covering up as much as before. However, that is a sham–failing to disclose all the useful information is another form of lying.

- *Partial disclosure.* Majority of cheater will tell only a part of the truth or tell outright lies to the betrayed partner. Typically, this partial disclosure will lead to the couple revealing to each other some information today, another tomorrow, the following day, et cetera. Over time, it becomes very painful for the betrayed partner besides rereading havoc in the process of rebuilding trust.

- *Child's role.* In this case, the offender plays the child, whereby he/she tells the betrayed partner, "there is something I need to tell you" then waits for the other person to ask "what is it" or "is that all" or "are you sure that is all." Instead of restoring the relationship, such inquisitions turn honesty into an investigation.

- *Minimizing.* Sometimes, a cheater is rigorously honest, but at the same time, he/she is trying to de-escalate or dismiss or minimize the reactions of their betrayed partners. They even do this out of love and most pure feelings because they do not want to see their partners suffer. However, the feeling is part of the healing process for a betrayed spouse, so trying to protect him/her is quite pointless. The cheater initiated the pain in the first place so he/she should allow it to take place.

- *Getting defensive or attacking.* Majority of the betrayed mates get angry when they hear the truth about the actions of the spouse. As such, the cheater takes the defensive side, and when faced with danger, he/she attacks. A form of attack can be blaming the spouse having brought on the affair. Although the cheater might be justified to feel defensive, this reaction is counteractive to a relationship building process. When and if a cheater says something like 'Yes, but...' in response, the purpose of the conversation changes.

- *Expecting instant forgiveness.* Some cheater will be rigorously honest with the expectation that opening up will earn them instance forgiveness. In most cases, that does not work. The betrayed person has to feel the whole process of betrayal and healing before he/she can forgive fully.

The first and most important step to rebuilding trust is to be entirely honest and live in a glass house, where the betrayed partner can see everything that is happening. The partner who cheated should ensure that he/she can account for every move he/she makes in a day and tell the partner all the details. If a cheater becomes fully open without complaining or being defensive, the betrayed partner will come around gradually.

Rigorous honesty is not easy, and most people caught cheating do not like it. It can be emotionally painful for the two partners. However, they will have to bear with it because it is a large part of healing and forgiveness. The good news is that, gradually, the cheated-on partner will develop confidence in the person who hurt him/her and believe that he/she is living an honest life once again.

Chapter 14: Dealing with Your Partner Obsession

If a couple decides to move on after a case of infidelity, certain things might take place. The betrayed person will feel hurt, exploited, uncherished, insecure, and among others, unsure. He/She might be willing to work on the relationship but then feel afraid that the person who cheated is not worthy of trust. A betrayed partner often questions the validity of the relationship, the things he/she believed about the partner, the future, the purpose of life with the spouse, et cetera.

As such, the betrayed person will need time to heal and rebuild the trust he/she had in the spouse. Openness will mean that the partner who betrayed the other will have to live in an open, trustable life, while the betrayed one verifies that there is nothing more to worry about. Sometimes, the betrayed and healing partner will become or appear to become obsessed with the verification process—asking endless questions, wanting to track every move, getting suspicious at the slightest provocation, and so on.

The cheater will have to understand the partner's need to be sure before trusting again. The willingness to bear with the obsessed person will show that the cheater values the spouse and the relationship thus rebuild the trust at a faster pace.

Tug help deals with the obsession; the spouse who cheated should show qualities that are needed to rebuild trust.

Firstly, he/she should show sincerity which is normally defined as a mix of honesty and seriousness. Stay open and transparent with your partner in all ways to rebuild the trust. With sincere communication, the trust will develop.

Secondly, he/she should show consistency. In a relationship, consistency shows dependability and trust. The person who cheated should strive to keep a consistent and predictable pattern to show the betrayed person that he/she is trustworthy again.

Thirdly, the person should show integrity which is regarded as truthfulness and honesty. When a person has integrity, he/she does the right things in the right way and at the right time, adhering to the ethical and moral principles they are committed to by choice. Do not sugar coat things for each other, but be open and willing to try.

Fourthly, commitment is needed. The act of commitment will reassure the betrayed person that the spouse who cheated is willing to work for the relationship. Commitment also gives people the patience to work on the relationship even if healing and forgiveness are taking long. Besides, a committed couple will set goals together and strive to make them come true. They will aim to get back on track and support one another if anything does not appear right.

Chapter 15: How to Change from Destroyer to Healer

After discovering infidelity, the cheater and the betrayed person are both at risk of becoming destroyers. Each person can choose a side opposing the other, and instead of healing each other and the relationship, they destroy it further. Being a healer will need time, space, and a clear mind, as well as determination and commitment. The anger and hurt that a betrayed person feels can make him/her turn from a trusting and loving person to an angry and bitter person full of resentment. Betrayal will easily turn a good person into a cold destroyer. On the other hand, the person who cheated might be filled with shame, denial, and guilt. Instead of acknowledging these feelings, the betrayer might go into full defense or attack mode and bring the relationship to its knees.

A couple may also go into stress or depression after infidelity, and they might bring down everything they have worked for in a very short period. There have been cases where people went to jail because they did something harmful to their partners after discovering a case of infidelity. A large number of divorce cases occurs because of infidelity. Homes crumble after years of building. It is up to the couple to find out if they want to continue the relationship or end it.

If they want to move on apart, the decision should be accepted with love and selflessness. It should not be that any person seeks to revenge or destroy the other after a breakup. If the couple chooses to continue with the relationship and heal, they should look for ways to support one another and rebuild each other. The first step should be communication. Each person should state what he/she wants and does not want in the relationship. It is also advisable for the couple to give each other space if the emotions and feeling are running high in the negative direction. If the two people are still bitter about what happened, sexual intimacy should be put on hold until everyone is ready for it.

With the right communication, openness, finding out what the other person needs, forgiveness, and listening to each other, a couple can move from destroyers to healers. It's true that what happened cannot be undone, but the only good thing now is for the couple to look at and understand what they want. Being honest about your feelings will help you heal. Also, allow yourself to feel the emotions and feelings occupying your mind and body. Avoid going into denial.

Another crucial part of becoming a healer is ensuring that you take care of yourself physically. Some days, you will have a hard time waking up, strength will leave your body, your life will feel difficult, and you will not know what to do. Ensure that you eat, sleep, and exercise. As difficult as it might be, your body needs energy. If you have a family, including children, you will be needed to take care of them. The infidelity is a storm passing, while your family will stay forever. Ensure that you have the strength to serve them. Healing should take place mentally, physically, and emotionally. It may take some time, but with the right practices, you will move from destroyer to healer. You will be able to inspire other people who know what you have been through.

Chapter 16: Healing from an Affair/Infidelity, Together or Apart

Regardless of how bad a case of infidelity seems to be, anyone can heal. The person cheating and the cheated on have their scars, and both seek to heal. After deep thought and consideration, a couple can choose to keep the relationship or separate. Either way, the people involved have to heal to move on with their lives properly.

For the two people involved to heal from the damage that has already occurred, there is the need for brutal honesty from both sides, where the offended needs to ask all the questions he/she wants to know answers from, while the offender has to answer them honestly. If the relationship has suffered due to the affair, for instance, complete communication breakdown, healing will require a lot of reflection on what triggered the mess. The two people will also need to focus on what it would take to make the relationship better. The bright side is, if the two people believe that the relationship is worth fighting for, it will be easier to find a way back.

First, the couple has to look at the standing of things. This requires tough questions such as: *Is the affair over? Has the cheating partner ended it or just put things on hold until the drama cools down?* If the cheating partner is just pretending to have ended things to win the partner, then it would be better if he/she takes the heart of the spouse in hand and squeezes it hard. It will hurt less than the pretense. If the affair has been put to an end on a good note, the person who was hurt needs ongoing reassurance from the spouse for a while to rebuild the trust; there is no guessing the amount of time needed. During this time, the privacy that the cheating spouse had before the infidelity will be gone. The text messages, calls, emails, and information about whereabouts had to be placed on the table for scrutiny. That is the only way to rebuild trust.

Some of the questions that the couple can explore together to cover the topic of ending the affair may include:

- When and how did it end?
- How can we be sure that you will not go back to the affair?
- What evidence can I use to believe you?
- What will you do if the other person gets in touch?
- What have you done to ensure that the other person cannot get in touch with you?
- You choose to end the affair and fight for this relationship. That means it was not as worthy as the primary relationship. What can make the relationship worth going back to again?
- I am worried, scared, paranoid, suspicious, insecure, and unsure. I cannot trust you anymore, and I do not think I will see you as a good person ever again. How can you help me to rebuild what we had?
- What can you do to help me believe you and stop checking on your every move?

Secondly, check if there is genuine remorse of regret. Healing will only begin if the couple owns its mistakes. The person who cheated has to own what happened and show remorse for it. The person who got cheated on needs to check the contributions he/she might have made and own them. It will not be easy for the innocent person to understand the cheating spouse, but he/she has to look for a way. The cheater has to show remorse for the harm caused and for starting the affair. It is important at this point to ensure that there is a commitment to protect the relationship and let go of any external affairs above all else.

Some of the questions to ask at this juncture include:

- Do you regret the affair and what would you not like about it?
- If you had not been caught, would you still be having an affair?
- How do you feel about ending the affair?
- How do you feel about the effects of the affair in our relationship?
- What did you tell yourself to keep the affair going?
- How do you feel about it now?

Before choosing to end the relationship or go on with it, there are some questions you need to consider.

- Are there things in the relationship worth fighting for now?
- Is there another chance of love and reconnection?
- If we go on, will we have a real relationship or is this just a convenient way of meeting our shared goals?
- Is it love or will we be together for the sake of the children and other mutual interests?

There is no scientific, right, or perfect answer for these questions, but if one person wants a relationship for convenience while the other wants to love and intimacy, healing will not take place. The two spouses have to come up with a solution that allows both of them to heal.

If the two people stay in the relationship without a common ground, then it will only be a ground for resentment, loneliness, hatred, and bitterness. The next phase of life will be vulnerable. For the relationship to work, there is a need for compatibility.

The two people do not have to be the same, but they have to be compatible.

Another question to consider as you go through the healing process is if you genuinely want each other. Truthfully, people sometimes outgrow a relationship. Somewhere in the middle of the relationship, we might realize that our needs are too different and our spouses cannot meet them. In such cases, letting go of the relationship with strength, love, and honesty can be better than waiting for it to die a slow and bitter death.

Some of the questions to consider while checking if you still want to be with your spouse include:
- How do you feel about your spouse compared to the other person you had an affair?
- What do you miss about your spouse and the other person?
- How do you feel about your spouse?
- Do you still miss your spouse?
- Does his infidelity make you feel like you will never be able to have a valid relationship?
- Are you still afraid of losing your spouse? Do you think you are still worthy of his/her love?
- What is it about me that your spouse still wants?
- Which part of your relationship is worth fighting for now?
- What do you still want in your relationship?
- Can the rage, anger, and devastation we feel now change to positive feelings?

If you choose to stay, you need to learn how to forgive and move forward. For the two people to have a chance of healing and moving forward, if there will be any forgiveness, the involved people have to look at their contributions to the current situation. How did the two people end up where they are and how can they change the circumstances? This assessment does not mean that we excuse the person cheating; it is identifying a space where the relationship can regrow. If the two people are still insisting that they did all they could to keep the relationship strong, then there is no room for growth. However, if everyone looks at their failures and is willing to change, the relationship can live.

Let this healing opportunity be a time to focus your energy to honesty and open exploration of the causes of infidelity. It is not a time for blame games. Instead, you should take responsibility and work together for a better future. It will be hard to find an empowered and appropriate answer if you do not understand what triggered the infidelity in the first place. Understand the past to move towards the future.

It is true that the person who cheated delivered the final blow, but looking closer, you will realize that both of you played a hand in the downfall. Healing will only happen if both of you own the part. Owning mistakes will not excuse anyone rather; it will help to make some sense. Many hard conversations will take place.

If you are the one who was cheated on, you will be angry, hurt, and scared and you have every reason to feel that way. As much as you can, try to stay open to hear all the information and make it safe to consider all options. The information shared during such moments will be used to repair the holes and grow the relationship.

Somewhere along the way, a partner and the person he/she cheated with had information about the weaknesses of your relationship which you lacked. This information was so vital that it fueled an affair. It might have sustained the infidelity and drained your relationship. The cheating spouse and the person he/she had an affair with knew what they had that was lacking in the primary relationship. You as the cheated on spouse need to gather this information to make your relationship powerful again.

If you were the one cheating, there is the critical need for you to look with courage, honesty, and an open heart at what the affair was offering you. Chances are, it will be something you were missing from your primary relationship. It is not enough for you to fall on your flaws, insecurities, or deficiencies as excuses. Blaming and denial do not answer anything, and it will only drain the courage required to get the relationship rolling again.

Getting back together will require the two people to explore together:

- What did the affair give you that is lacking in our relationship?
- How did you feel in the affair that kept you going back? Did you feel more cherished? Loved? Are you wanted and desired? Nurtured? What can we add to our relationship to keep you from going back?
- What can I do to make you feel the way you felt in the affair?
- When did you feel the need to go out of our relationship?
- What had died in me?
- What is the difference between the other person and me?
- What would you like me to do more often? What would you like me to reduce?
- At this moment, the relationship is not working as it should. How can we improve it?
- Can we honestly meet the needs required for the relationship to thrive again?

When you understand what fueled the infidelity, you can then look at what the needs for your relationships are and if they can be met. Sometimes, people are not willing to even try rebuilding the relationship. Other times, the hurt, hatred, and resentment can be so much so that the spouses want separation. Both parties need to look at what they want from the relationship and also assess what they are willing to offer to move forward.

Sometimes, the rift arising between two people after a case of infidelity is so vast that it cannot be put together. If that is the case, accept it and decide openly and with courage and love to fight or not fight for the relationship knowing that it will be challenging. There is nothing as tiresome as fighting to hold on to someone or something that is not interested. If it is the case, be honest and save your energy. A relationship where someone has deep and important needs that are not being met will not be sustainable.

To the one who strayed: staying forgiven and getting closer.

If you are the one who had an affair, it is now time to guard your relationship and make boundaries. As with any traumatizing experience, finding out about an affair will generate a massive potential for re-experiencing the shocks over and over. Here is how: every time there is a gap or some form of unexplained event in your relationship, panic will set in. Any unanswered calls, missed texts, the phone off, getting a voice message, your location unknown, and you have not reported, your spouse will feel insecure. Any time you are not where you said you would be, you are home late without an explanation, you did not keep a promise you made, and any other thing that is associated with a continuing affair will make you answerable. There will be recurring feelings of betrayal, panic, anger, fear, sadness, loneliness, suspicion, loss, among others. The shocks of trauma will keep recurring, and they should not be hurried. Let everyone take their time to heal.

If you had an affair, you now must make your partner feel worthy and safe again. To facilitate this, ensure that you are 100% accountable such that your partner knows there is nothing hidden. The privacy you had before the affair is now gone for a while. Stay in a glass house where everything you do can be seen. Your partner might not have been the suspicious and paranoid type before you cheated but be sure he/she will own these traits for a while. That is what affairs cause. They turn loving, trusting, and open hearts to suspicious broken and resentful ones. Even the calmest people can turn wild at this moment. The length of time that the resentment period lasts is dependent on your openness.

Rebuilding the relationship will require big moves on your part. It might even mean quitting your job because the person you had an affair with is working in that office. Your partner has to be the priority in this case, and if he/she wants a tracking device on your phone for reassurance sake, you better be willing. It does not have to stay this way, but for now, every sacrifice is needed to reassure your spouse.

Be accountable every minute of the day. Stay open, and let there be no secrets. Knowing that you are honest and open will help the heart heal from trauma and anxiety that comes from discovering the affair. Your cheated-on spouse will look for information even though there is nothing to find out. The porpoise of looking is not to find but to make sure that there is nothing in secret. For wholesome healing to happen, it will be your turn to be responsible and stand in the guard of your relationship boundaries for a while.

Be accountable to the extent that there are no gaps, no missing pieces, and no absences in the day. There should be no secrets. If the person you cheated with contacts you, make sure that you report to your partner before he/she even gets suspicious. Be on the frontline to make things safe again. For the betrayed person, there will be the need to find reassurance and evidence that the affair is not taking place anymore. This need might last for years, and it might even appear like an obsession. Finding out about a case of infidelity is very traumatizing, and the only way a betrayed person will recover is by searching for proof that the partner is truthful and the relationship is safe.

For the betrayed person:

Forgive yourself first: for feeling angry, for feeling sad, for doubting yourself. Forgive yourself for being hateful and even contemplating revenge. Forgive yourself for not realizing that things are wrong in the relationship. Forgive yourself for not taking the right steps as soon as you noticed something was wrong. Let go of the feeling of self-doubt, shame, mistrust. Forgive yourself for wanting to leave and wanting to stay. Forgive yourself for the feelings you felt before the affair and after.

Every relationship has its ups and downs. There is a make it or break it point for every two people in a commitment. Some relationships will have one weak point while others will have limitless. Your relationship involved two people, and if your partner felt unfulfilled, it was up to him/her to tell you and ask for support. If he/she asked and you were not attentive, then forgive yourself and take the lesson. There might have been times when your needs went unfulfilled too, but you did not choose to stray. These unfulfilled moments will happen in every relationship once in a while. It is the duration and intensity that marks the difference in damage. The longer a person has to wait, the higher the chances for cheating. You deserve the opportunity to know when things are not right; therefore, find a cure. You deserve the chance to repair the developing holes. You are getting it now as you work on your healing. Forgive yourself if you do not have the chance to give your partner what he/she needs henceforth. Sometimes, a great relationship will not occur even if you offer all you have. Sometimes, the relationship will not fail just because one person is broken; rather, it is the combination of the two people.

Everyone in the world is another person's idea of perfect. There is someone out there who looks at you and thinks you are beautiful. Probably, your partner has seen you like that since he/she met you, but somewhere along the way, things fell apart. At this moment though, you are feeling traumatized and a series of feelings you cannot explain. It is okay, give yourself time to heal, forgive, focus, and refocus. It might take a while to start feeling okay again even if you choose to end the relationship. Be patient and kind to yourself. You have been through a lot.

Conclusion

And finally...

Thank you for making it through to the end of *Healing from Infidelity: A Practical Guide to Healing from Infidelity and How to Help Your Partner to Heal from Your Affair*. Let us hope it was informative and has provided you with the tools you need.

Not every affair will mark the end of a relationship. However, every case of infidelity will redefine a relationship. There will be anger and hurt, and both spouses will feel lost and lonely for a while. If you feel that your relationship is worth continuing and is worth fighting for, there will be plenty of room for rediscovering and growth with the right guidance and steps.

The heartache will not always feel stronger than you. Some days you will feel sad, while others you will be as strong as ever. This alteration of moods is fine because you are grieving–for what you had, what you thought you were working for, and what you are losing. You are in doubt of who you thought you were. You are not sure about your spouse anymore. Everything is there, but you are wondering if it is the same. Sometimes, it is not better or worse. It is just different.

Good people make bad decisions, and anyone can be a victim of bac choices anytime. It is hard to explain why we end up hurting the people we love the most. Sometimes, we become the people we never imagined we could be. The good thing about mistakes is that they instill in our cores new truths and wisdom we would not necessarily know. An affair or case of infidelity is a tough time for any relationship, but it does not have to be its definition. Rather than gathering the broken pieces and going over and over them to keep the wounds fresh, we can use what we have to make a better life for ourselves and spouses. Knowledge is power, and it can be used to make the relationship stronger, wiser, more knowledgeable, honest, and full of more sustainable love.

Printed in Great Britain
by Amazon